Silent

Barbara Erakko Taylor

Silent Dwellers

EMBRACING THE

SOLITARY LIFE

CONTINUUM   NEW YORK

1999

The Continuum Publishing Company
370 Lexington Avenue
New York, NY 10017

Printed in the United States of America

Library of Congress Cataloging-in-Publication Data

Taylor, Barbara Erakko, 1947–
    Silent dwellers : embracing the solitary life/Barbara Erakko Taylor
        p.   cm.
    ISBN 0-8264-1212-2 (pbk.: alk. paper)
    1. Spiritual life—Catholic Church.   2. Solitude—Religious aspects—
Catholic Church. I. Title.
    BX2350.2.T39   1999
    248.4'7—dc21   99-26259
                                              CIP

To

Bp. P. Francis Murphy
for listening to God speaking
in human words
with kindness and love

Fr. Richard H. Tillman
for nurturing me and many others
in our spiritual journeys

Jim Gerofsky
for writing the letter that
prompted this book

and

the Solitaries
who dwell among us in silence

Contents

Introduction

It has been a couple of years since I have written about myself as a solitary in *Silence: Making the Journey to Inner Quiet*. In that time, the unabomber has been apprehended. When I read about him, I said to myself and others, "Now *that* is a hermit." I could not imagine such solitude. Living for weeks alone without seeing another human being, eating nothing but vegetables out of a garden, riding a rusty bicycle into town and back, having no friends, and speaking only with the most distancing politeness to merchants.

Solitude leads to insanity or spiritual health. There is no middle road. Nor is the hermit well understood by society. The vocation resides in the deepest heart of every religion, as well as in every psychiatric ward. By definition, it is enigmatic. Only when—and if—the hermit comes back wiser is there any "proof" of the spiritual authenticity of, and need for, the solitary.

What does the modern-day Christian hermit contribute to the Body of Christ?

An authentic call to solitude has the same criteria—inner peace and certitude—as a call to any other vocation. Spiritual direction is crucial because solitude is unusual. It goes against the biological urge to live in community. It is hard to live in unrelenting aloneness. And, emotional problems and life trauma can easily beguile us into thinking that God is calling us out of society.

But, rather than fleeing from the active church community and an active ministry, the person truly called to a solitary lifestyle is drawn into the hiddenness of God *for the sake of community*. In the face of the seeming meaninglessness of their withdrawal, they express an unshakable belief that solitude—like the space between a heartbeat—is essential to the Church.

The solitary, without cognitive understanding, retains an extraordinary trust in God that this offering of silence somehow unites and strengthens the Church. The hermit treads a path, alone, to God. And God, in kindness, will meet the solitary in ways we will never know.

In spite of the unusualness of a call to solitude, it is a vocation not peopled by saints but by mere people. People leading solitary lives become cranky, angry, fearful, lazy, and as tempted by distractions from God as any other Christian. They no more perfectly walk the path of solitude than a teacher teaches his or her first class with perfect compassion and authority.

*   *   *

When I felt a certainty that God was calling me to a solitary life, I began to search for others who could guide me.

My first problem was in simply *believing* what was in my heart—that I had, in fact, a hermit's vocation. I—who loved to talk. I—who grew fearful, intensely so, of separating myself from the approval of society. I—who wanted to be alone in nature, but was terrified of being raped, robbed, or killed—or without instant medical assistance.

I wanted a guidebook—a self-help book.

I soon found that, while the saints frequently left behind

spiritual self-help books, hermits did not. The Desert Fathers, renowned for their wise and pithy truths, left suggestions. But they spoke of desert asceticism—"Go, sit in your cell, and your cell will teach you everything"—not suburban possibilities for today's women and men. How, I wondered, could solitude be fruitful today— if the person lived in a congestion-clogged city, or a tract-home suburb and was not sure she had the guts for isolated wilderness?

The most well-known guide to the modern solitary life, I found, was Thomas Merton. He spent most of his Trappist life unearthing the ancient traditions supporting solitude within the Church, but he actually lived it very little. Death intervened.

Merton seemed almost genetically wired to hunger for solitude. Once it erupted within him, it was the constant goad that drove his life. One could say that his deepest nature was solitary. Yet, ironically, this desire was implanted in a brilliant, gifted, extroverted communicator. Society valued, nurtured, and preferred the tangible gifts of his writing over the intangible possibilities of his solitude.

He never became the hermit he wished to be. While he inspired thousands to trust the hunger for the deeply contemplative life, possibly even a solitary one, he could not provide that weathered hard-knock-school-of-experience handbook for a modern age.

I also looked to the mystics. Through the centuries, they had written about the interior castle, the diamond, the *via negativa*—all acknowledging the solitary nature of God plunging into one's soul. But for the most part, the mystics lived in community. Was there, I wondered, a subtle distinction between the call of the mystic and the call of the hermit? The mystic feels, albeit intermittently, the *presence* of God—and for them, that *is* God. The hermit feels the presence of *silence*, and for the hermit, *that* is God. For the true solitary, community— even silent community—blocks the silence-that-is-God because it provides a comfort, and therefore a distraction, from the call to utter aloneness with God. The unique trademark of the hermit is the need for physical separation. It did not seem that the mystical literature would answer the questions of a modern-day solitary.

*   *   *

The solitaries in today's society first have to contend with their illusions about ideal solitude. When the call first erupts, they most likely are entirely enmeshed in the infrastructure of society. For example, houses themselves are designed to enable the residents to interact—both within the walls, and outside them. One contemplative friend and I once considered sharing her house. As I slowly studied its architecture, I realized it would be impossible. The rooms all opened onto common corridors; the bathrooms were centrally located; the main traffic pattern of the house was through the kitchen/family area, and the spectacular views were built around the living room.

In order to perpetuate itself, society must provide structures that encourage interaction, and that need is literally built into the walls. Homes, whether apartment, town house, or separate dwelling, teach future generations how to live together. For the solitary, every aspect is wrong. The hermit wants a minimal dwelling that architecturally *discourages* interaction and community.

In my suburban house, I have too many rooms, too many possessions, and too much maintenance. The phone rings too often. The gutters fall off. The sewers clog. The rooms need painting. The sink needs to be replaced. Solitude in the suburbs is not cheap—nor is it free from the daunting impositions of maintenance time. I have often considered fleeing to the country—but have never received the inner peace and clarity to do so.

*   *   *

Almost immediately, people drawn to solitude realize that their health will depend heavily upon their relationship to the nature around them. In the absence of human companionship, it is nature that comforts and consoles and teaches. For suburban hermits, that nature is small, tame, and bounded by hedges and sidewalks, ornamental gates, and mulched garden beds. It is intimate. They must kneel down and touch the leaves of one bush. They know the moss growing in the nook of the tree, the ivy climbing up a stone, which weeds blossom by the nearby creek also overrun by teenage trash. One leaf can open them into the comforting embrace of silence.

But there may be no solitude unless you walk early in the morning or late at night. The children come tumbling out in all ages and sizes to talk to you. The teenage girl will join your entire walk, chewing gum and talking about her prom dress and boyfriend. The neighbor will walk down the street and knock on your door if you fail to answer your phone.

So, in the suburbs, the hermit must learn how to find his or her way through society's door into God's embrace. Solitaries must accept it and acknowledge its rules. They will enter into solitude as a pruned bonsai, continually trimmed by society.

But not every solitary lives within dense populations. There is wild untamed solitude of the mountains and valleys, forests and streams, meadows and farmlands. I have not lived in that solitude, except occasionally. It is a strong, dense silence. The length and breadth and width of your desire for solitude unfurls, unimpeded by society, until your own fear gathers it up again.

Each solitary's story is unique. Each story is lived alone.

*   *   *

After nearly ten years of desire, and seven years of lived solitude, I have a more realistic view of how to nurture solitude slowly in a suburban setting. I owe much of the credit to my nonhermit friends who sometimes incredulously watched me try to fly solitarily, only to flop and crash, severely miscalculating my ability to "be alone."

Mature Christians, even if not called to solitude themselves, provide essential ballast to the solitary. They watch with an attentive caring eye. Their comments, all too often, are right on target. Frequently I have had to back away from the extreme to a more gradual interpretation of solitude in the midst of society.

Having no guidebook, or "rules," I presumed upon God. As a result of a week-long retreat taken in 1993, I wrote, under the blanket of prayer, a Covenant of Hope.

*   *   *

To my surprise, it has not only supported me in my solitude these past five years, it has strengthened and defined it.

At the time I wrote it, the presence of some of the vows surprised even me. What did solidarity have to do with solitude? How could I be "obedient?" Obedient to whom? Others seemed essential—silence, solitude, simplicity, prayer. Later, to my chagrin, a friend asked where the vow of celibacy was, and only then did I realize it was missing. Why was that?

COVENANT OF HOPE

I seek union with God in the spirit of Carmel through silence, solitude, simplicity, solidarity, obedience, and prayer that I may love properly.

Silence: To choose communion with God over my own voices.

Solitude: To choose solitude as a dwelling place for God over my own desire for society.

Simplicity: To choose to give rather than receive.

Solidarity: To choose oneness with the poor and dispossessed by becoming poor and dispossessed.

Obedience: To honor the obligations of my life over my own preferences.

Prayer: To be in God's presence always.

I enter freely into this covenant with the desire to live it for the remainder of my life.

*   *   *

I have thought—and lived—deeply into my solitude. There are insights that come from unrelenting solitude—and unrelenting intrusions *into* solitude. Both are problematic for the solitary.

The solitary life does not come easy. When I deeply accept

my vocation, I am like a hidden spring that pours forth—in writing, in prayer, in love. And when I resist it, I am like a whimpering truculent child. As I grow very slowly into this solitary life, I too am faced with temptations. I can fall in love. I can get aroused sexually. I want movies and distractions. I want to run from God. Especially in the beginning, I looked for a hole through the hedge of my vocation where I could emerge, once again, as a socially acceptable woman. Wife. Mother. Church volunteer. Friend. Someone would give me the magic key, the missing piece of the puzzle—and it would all be okay. I would be "normal."

But more than my desire for normalcy was a desire to live in the very bowels of the silent unknowable God. People drawn to solitude at some point step across a boundary into their vocation. I did make a choice. It was right for me. And though I will perhaps never *completely* accept it—for it is an enigma—as the years go by I see that I allow it to form me and I trust it more deeply.

There are solitaries who live quietly in our midst, but do not write. Not having the lived experience of decades of solitude, I offer (as the Buddhists say) the beginner's mind. It is perhaps helpful to someone increasingly drawn to solitude and facing the same questions I once faced. If I wrote as an expert, it would perhaps be too daunting—even for me.

When solitude is seen as extraordinary, then it seems to require extraordinary courage. Eventually, however, it becomes ordinary. Stripped of illusion and delusion, it is simply a lifestyle that contributes to the Body of Christ in an ordinary, everyday way.

It is in that context I offer this book.

Silence

To Choose Communion with God
over My Own Voices

When I began to build my life in solitude, I was very intent upon keeping my mind focused on God, in accordance with the contemplative mystical tradition. I structured the silence. I spent time on prayer, scripture, reading, writing, and work. I thought the eremitic path replicated the mystic path, only one was always solitary while the other was not necessarily so.

I chose "communion with God over my own voices." And those voices were many.

The key pitfall, I quickly learned, was the word "over." I was determined to use my disciplined will *over* this incessant internal chatter to subdue it, like corralling wild horses into a tiny fenced pasture. I appropriated the rules of contemplative communities such as the Trappists, Carthusians, and Carmelites for my own suburban hermitage. My understanding was that one *applied* oneself to the task. One *worked* to create an environment for mystical communion with God.

Accordingly, when I first began my silence, I tried to keep my mind always directed towards God. I wanted to build an artificial tower of silence, on my terms, by my definition of holiness and honor and praise to our God. Higher and higher the tower went, more intense, more scrupulous, more disciplined.

It could not survive.

Its demise came when I left my hermitage one year later, hungering for the natural beauty of our national parks. I visited beautiful parks and forests. I traveled along coastlines and lakes. In mountains and across deserts. Suddenly my man-made silence counted for nothing. The silence of nature overwhelmed me.

When I returned home, all I could do was sit. My efforts to be holy in silence were shown, by the silent mountain, the roaring sea, the toneless desert, to be the man-made dead ends they were.

I was so overwhelmed, I fell silent. I fell, not into the silence of mountains or starry nights or dew-drenched flowers—but into the silence of *humans,* where endless thoughts, calm and tumultuous, flow from first breath of life to last.

The structured day allowed little time for random thoughts to float around. As a result, when I went to bed, they could overwhelm me, wresting sleep from me. After I abandoned such strict discipline, those same thoughts tumbled through the silence all day long like sagebrush on a prairie. But when I lay down to sleep at night, I easily fell asleep. It seemed that I needed a certain amount of time to be in "thought."

I began to feel there might be a distinct difference between solitary solitude—and its needs—and communal silence.

The contemplative-in-community may work, eat, and pray in silence—but that silence is vibrant with unspoken energy. One feels comforted by the loving presence of others, even if words are not spoken. Or, if there is strife in the community, one feels that pain and anguish even in utter silence.

The community contemplative seeks to discipline the will toward God within communal silence; but it is physical silence itself that disciplines the hermit.

In my experience, physical silence works slowly, like water flowing over a stone. It will draw the solitary into deeper quietness without any force. As long as the hermit clings to his or her dwelling, leaving it only for the necessary or meaningful requirements of human life, silence will become the teacher.

Silence may be slow, but its work is inexorable. I fear I could not survive within a religious community. I have the will for silence, but little else.

Silence, for me, was not a path to something—it was both the beginning and the end of my desire. It was the silence of earth, bound in time and space and teeming with my inner voices in which I began to feel the deepest sense of the hidden presence of God. As though God accompanied me through all moments, not just the timeless, spaceless ones.

I cannot express how much this subtle difference surprised me. I strove so hard to discipline myself like a bride preparing for her espousal, but it went against my nature. I was more content to let the inner voices simply babble while I enjoyed—relished—physical silence. So I have always had noise within; silence without. I imagine many mystics, slowly advancing on their destined path, have silence within; noise without. They can move about freely in the world, carrying their union with God within them like a turtle within its shell.

After my travels, I abandoned discipline. I became erratic in my daily practices. I looked at each day individually, and listened within to see what was needed to relate to this silence within me. Slowly, new patterns have emerged.

To quiet one's voice, to quiet one's lifestyle, to quiet one's dwelling—each of these moves one in a different way into silence. One mustn't hurry this union with silence. It is difficult and hard, and I have remained at shallow plateaus for long times. Fear must be dealt with at every stage.

Silencing the voice can mean many things. To not speak, to speak softly, to speak more slowly, to be more observant of thoughts disturbing silence. I continue to have a divided personality. I am "on" or "off." I talk fast and loud and exuberantly; or I am utterly silent in my own solitude. I sense that deepening silence will harmonize these extremes within me. When I *feel* silent all the time, regardless of whether I am talking or not, then I will be in harmony with that silence.

In the beginning, even though I lived alone, I chattered. I woke up talking to myself, to the dog, to the plants, to the refrigerator. I had conversations—silent and often aloud. Especially with my dog. When I walked her, I talked nonstop. I had a dialogue with a dog.

One day I realized that even though I was alone, I was not silent. So I stopped talking to the dog. I thought she would notice it. Perhaps she did. But we made the transition successfully. Now I get the leash—which is better than any command—hook her collar, and open the door. Not one word is said between us in the morning or the evening. She is in absolute reverie with her world; I with mine.

Physical silence can be very dense. When you live utterly alone, it must carry you—or you will go stark raving mad with loneliness. It takes a special kind of letting go to trust that this is your path, that God will come to you in this human void.

I think it is more akin to the watery world of a mother's womb, rather than a handshake with God.

There is also a pace within our lifestyle that allows silence to remain present and conscious within us. We can microwave a single-portion Weight Watcher dinner, or we can quietly chop vegetables, cook brown rice, and saute fish. We can set dead-lines that may seem slow by normal work-world standards, but are still too fast for silent dwellers. We can have a large wardrobe, with all its attendant decisions, or a small one.

I have quieted my lifestyle, or perhaps it was an inevitable consequence of living in silence. Things slipped away—the desire for prepared food, alcohol, caffeine, and sugar, the need for a wardrobe, the yearning for multimedia entertainment. They are not eliminated, but the craving is less. It is as though I eat silence; I wear silence; I hear silence—and that fills my body and soul.

A silent dwelling is a simple dwelling. Fewer—but not too few—possessions, each one somehow drawing its owner into silence. I have an inverted glass pyramid vase in which I float a single carnation. The flower stays fresh for seven days. That one flower on a simple table draws me into silence. Each piece of furniture adds to my silence by its own beauty and quietness. Slowly I am divesting myself of things I once thought would quiet me, but in the end distract me. Too many books. Art. Subscriptions. Inherited furniture. Impulse-bought souvenirs.

Every day I spend some time cleaning and divesting my dwelling of clutter. I am inefficiently slow at this, but the task itself is a comforting silence, one that quietly engrosses me.

I wonder if that deeper silence comes more frequently to those who slow their lifestyle down to a pace where silence can steal in, unnoticed, and slip away.

I don't deliberately seek such moments, but I think they may be more frequent since I am not time-compressed to finish a task because three more lie ahead of it. Each task, for the quiet solitary, is a beginning and an end. There is a spaciousness because so many things have been removed from one's life, one's calendar.

The mind is less cluttered by memories and fears. The thoughts, always present, are like a constant stream of bit players on open mike night—but in an empty theater. These background thoughts affect me like seasonings in a stew. They create the mood of my silence.

That is the silence of a hermit. The solitary watches the mind flow of thoughts, wrapped in God's protective heart. The silence itself is vibrant and multitextured. It is dense some days, so heavy and gray—black really—that the solitary can hardly move. And then some days, the silence is brilliant, crystalline with the beauty of sheer joy. But most days are a little cloudy, with splatters of radiant sun, gently overcast, or quietly light.

Everything is intensified in silence. The human emotions of anger, hope, fear, anguish, love, and joy live also within the heart of the hermit. Nothing is concealed in silence. When my mind is fraught with these emotions, I sit in silence. I do not hurry them along. Emotions, I have found, have their own pathway. They will guide you into your own soul, if you allow them the space and time of silence.

I have a cockatiel that recently died. She died while I was away one day, and it seemed a violent death. It was premature. She was lying on the bottom of her cage, her neck seemingly broken as though she had endured terrible suffering as she died.

For four years, she had shepherded me through my first years of solitude, often bobbing on my hand while I typed, or throwing paper clips off my desk.

When I saw her, wings outstretched, neck twisted, eyes frozen open, I fell into a silence so deep and unimaginable that I did not move from her cage for a timeless time. The emotions of anguish, horror, sorrow, guilt, and love swirled inward into the silence. I did nothing. I thought little.

For one day, I grieved in the bottomless depths of silence. Then I wrapped her and buried her and went on with my life.

Some emotions within us are so molten they feel as though they are burning our soul to charred cinders. I sit through these storms. The longest I have ever sat is three days. If I fought the emotion, or denied it, I think it would fester and infect my spirit worse. It seems better to let the hurt run through you like a river flood than to resist it. Silence is a balm stronger than any wound.

Silence, to me, is to do no violence to the thoughts coursing through. It is a subtle thing. I listen to them with God's heart. God watches over us the way I watch over my thoughts—as a protective mother. The mother does not stop the child from playing on the sliding board. She feels the emotions of the child. She is excited, horrified, ready in an instant, to rescue. It is the same with thoughts. I hold them in the playground of my mind, giving them space and time to live out their stories. Sometimes I enjoy them. Other times I am horrified by them. But there is the slight separation of mother from child. I am not one with them. I am, however, one with the emotion of them. And emotion, like water, flows. So I sit with them, or add a prayer to their serene or turbulent waters.

What makes the hermit an enigma to society is that the solitary seems to surrender all the joys of being a human for a Don Quixote quest.

She accepts physical silence *and* the turbulence of unholy thoughts as being the spot where God is *most* present. The hermit almost suspects ecstasy as being self-delusion. The sign of the solitary is hiddenness, not only from society but from oneself. No one can clearly see his or her own self. In time, I suspect the silent dweller ceases trying. Incapable of understanding or explaining their yearning, the solitary eventually chooses to surrender such issues to God, preferring silence to even human comprehension.

Yet the solitary is also the most hopeful of individuals. In order to live in silence, the hermit has to believe, absolutely, that God *wants* this useless exercise of solitary silence. That it somehow contributes to the *communion* of people.

The silent dweller sees fruit where no one else sees it: delight in a weedy flower, compassion for a tired mother scolding her child, inward contentment beneath an overcast day. The murdered and the murderer, the starved and the oppressor—the solitary sees some strange rhythm recurrent in all of us, an ebb and flow of dark and light playing upon the human soul.

In order for society to function, sound as well as silence is needed. The solitary merely points, with his life, to that need. Their life is an iconlike statement of the pause between the heartbeat of life, without which no meaningful life can occur.

That is the Don Quixote quest for the silent dweller.

Solitude

To Choose Solitude as a Dwelling Place for God
over My Own Desire for Society

I live alone. I live physically separated from others. This is solitude. It is voluntarily removing oneself for a lengthy period of time from the mainstream of societal interaction. Why?

No one can know, with absolute certainty, that hunger for solitude is driven solely by the Spirit. We have an infinite number of ways of deceiving ourselves.

There is always the caveat—that the hermit has withdrawn because of unresolved personal issues. In that case, solitude offers an opportunity for reflection and renewal and reentry. But if it is a vocational call, those same issues will be resolved within the solitude, and the solitude itself will deepen.

No one should attempt solitude in emotional isolation. Deep friendships are essential; and good spiritual direction, if it can be found, is invaluable. The solitary is not in isolation, but rather in the hidden heart of community.

Solitude, by definition, invites one inward. Those voluntarily entering it will repeatedly and frequently ask if they are engaged in non-Christ-like navel gazing, and forgoing the kingdom of God. The answer will never be resolutely clear.

I have lived alone for seven years, but it is an aloneness contained within a bustling suburban community. My aloneness is not isolation. There are children playing in the streets; parents going to and from work; lawn mowers growling on weekends; barbecues going. My aloneness is contained within that milieu.

It takes time to resolve the ideal with the reality. Many silent dwellers today must work for a living. They may live in apartments, rented rooms, or houses. Occasionally I will read of a man or woman who has gone into the mountains and lived a primitive life. Sometimes I hear that they come back, exhausted by the enormous physical labor required to sustain themselves in such an environment.

It is easy to miss the meaning and purpose of solitude, and thereby misinterpret it.

When I initially designed a solitary lifestyle, I chose a small brick house in a suburban community, to be near my children. It never occurred to me that I would find suburban living restrictive and contrary to this silence I sought. I assumed that four solid brick walls would provide me with the hermitage I wanted. Yet, as the initial year passed, I began to feel trapped in this complex societal infrastructure, and I wanted to flee.

I dreamed of leaving the area, of finding an acre or two and building a small four-room house. I searched the newspaper for ads, drove to distant places looking for this wilderness Shangri-La. I felt I could not become a real hermit without it. I was being stifled by neighbors constantly wanting to chat, cars going up and down the street, the telephone ringing, and friends' insistence that I maintain some social contact with them.

I ended up buying an RV. It was my "hermitage on wheels." I abandoned the monetarily simple life, and complicated it by adding a second house. Then I drove it all over the country—from Maryland to Colorado, from Maryland to Florida, from Maryland to Minnesota. Then I sold it for an older, cheaper one I found in Washington state and drove that one home across the entire United States. Altogether I spent nearly three months on the road in my quest for absolute solitude in a wilderness setting.

Only then did I come to a deeper understanding of solitude.

There is an old story about a poor Jewish family whose house was filled with children and pets. The father went to the rabbi and said, "It is noisy all the time. I have no quiet in my house." And the rabbi said, "Put your goat in the house." The man could not believe his ears, but he trusted the rabbi and did as he was told. The noise got worse. He came back, and said, "Rabbi, it's worse than ever." And the rabbi said, "Bring the chickens in." And incredulous though he was, he still trusted the rabbi. He brought the hens into the house. The crowing and cackling drove him crazy. He went back to the rabbi. This time, the rabbi told him to bring the cow into the house. Now the tiny house was filled with five children, a cat, two dogs, a goat, eleven chickens, and a milk cow. The man had it. He went to the rabbi in a rage. "I came to you needing quiet, and my house is worse than ever. What good is your advice?" Then the rabbi said, "Take the cow, and chickens, and goat out of the house." The man, relieved, went home and did as the rabbi said. The next time he saw him, he said, "Rabbi, you'll never believe it. My house is so quiet."

When I came home from the last trip, exhausted and lonely, my home finally became a hermitage. A dwelling becomes solitary when its owner believes it is so. A solitary dwelling is the place one can relax into deepest silence. The purpose of solitude is to invite quietness into your life. If you are constantly stressed, fretful, worried, or exhausted, then your current situation is not the right place for solitude.

It was my idealism—my wanting to be an austere hermit—that made me disparage my home. In wanting to please God, and gain some assurance that I was being faithful to what I perceived as a call to solitude, I saw only one expression of aloneness. That of the wilderness dweller. The desert father. The woman chopping wood for a snowbound winter. The little house on the prairie.

I came home from my last RV experience desperate for the solitude and security of my own dwelling place. It was as though I finally bonded to my hermitage. I realized how much the hermit needs to "nest" by not moving about excessively. I settled in for a winter of consolation.

Solitude implies not only a dwelling but a state of mind.

One of the biggest issues for the person desiring solitude concerns one's interactions with society. If one has been living a normal modern lifestyle, the modes of engaging in relationships are numerous. There are friends and social engagements, meetings and volunteer work, work and vacation. To keep in touch, there are answering machines, E-mail addresses, and fax machines, cellular phones and pagers, call forwarding, call waiting, and caller ID.

One has to want solitude *more* than all of these. There are certainly "time-outs" when anyone leading an active lifestyle retreats to a secluded setting, leaving behind the job and friends, the phone and pager. But if one wants to permanently live in solitude, the issue will strike at the very core of your definition of society.

The calendar and the telephone are the barometer.

I began by asking for a sabbatical from all of my volunteer activities. This was easily understood, as all of us get burned out. It allowed me to keep one foot in, one foot out. I was not at all sure, initially, that I had any real call to solitude. Within a few months, everyone forgot about me. Truly. We seem so invaluable, but out of sight quickly equates to out of mind.

The telephone presented another problem entirely. Its raucous ring breaks solitude into a thousand pieces. There are two ways to look at this. The desert fathers cordially greeted all who came. If they became too popular, they took their sparse possessions and simply moved to another secret place and began again.

If today's solitary views incoming telephone calls as a hermit form of desert hospitality, callers will invite themselves—by telephone, E-mail, fax, or answering machine—into the hermitage. For the caller, it is a natural societal interaction. For the solitary, always at home, it is hospitality—or trespass.

The modern-day hermit can rely on an answering machine, but then he or she is required to return calls, which is the delayed equivalent of receiving it directly.

I think a major reason I was looking for a wilderness Shangri-La was because I failed to realize the enormous impact of modern communications upon solitude. It was a radical move simply to turn off the telephone ringer for lengthy periods of time.

This I have done. But I also have an aging mother, and friends, and doctors, dentists, and business contacts. How do I allow controlled access into my solitude?

I wear a pager at all times for family emergencies, and regularly check my answering machine for messages. To my surprise, I found that by dividing and separating the modes of interaction, the phone is, at last, silenced. The pager soundlessly vibrates when the family needs me. Doctors, business associates, family, and close friends leave messages on the answering machine.

When the phone finally fell silent, my home truly became a hermitage. I no longer felt I had to move in order to attain solitude.

Lastly, there is E-mail and the Internet.

The Internet has no agenda. It is a morally indifferent container of all that constitutes human communication and thought. It does not need our companionship with it in order to exist. The fascination it holds for us, however, is immense. Like an endless game of solitaire, it begs you to turn the next card, to click the hand icon on the next image or keyword.

I recently wanted a national newspaper address, and ended up clicking on, and reading, *Takoma Park Voice*—the city paper for my birth home. In that instance, my focused solitude was lost. But it was not the Internet that intruded into and disrupted my lifestyle; it was my own intoxication with knowledge—even knowledge for which I had no need.

Coupled with moments of loneliness—and the opportunity to join spiritual discussion groups—the Internet can become a siren seducing the most determined solitary to abandon inner silence.

E-mail, on the other hand, is an auditorially silent answering machine. The main "noise" is one of quantity. I have waited for the past few years to see the fallout from this new mode of communicating. People joke that they are now mass-deleting unread messages. They complain of the extra time it takes to sift through them. That doesn't mean E-mail is not for the solitary, only that the address is as precious as an unlisted phone.

For the modern solitary, the quest for silence has vastly broader boundaries than what one's predecessors faced. Solitude is real only when it is relative to the world in which it is lived. It is unreal if attempted in fantasy—as though telephones and fax machines, the Internet and E-mail did not exist.

Today, my calendar is spacious. I belong to three faith-sharing groups, some beginning in pre-solitude days. These are the friends who can nurture my solitude. I do prison ministry once a month. Prisoners know a confined solitude in a way that free society cannot. I attend Mass every Sunday. I see my mother twice a week. There are occasional doctors' appointments, shopping chores, and I will enjoy a movie or a dinner out one or two times a month. Altogether, I am in my hermitage perhaps 70 to 80 percent of the time.

I relish and enjoy time with others. I have been called "the sociable hermit." Ironically, lengthy solitude often invokes a verbal avalanche when I find myself with a dear and treasured friend, or at a rare social occasion. I sound like the windup energizer non-stop-talking bunny. Solitaries, I suppose, are not always introverts. But I wind down quickly, by social standards, and look fatigued and worn two hours later.

I have not yet learned how to carry solitude and silence into the marketplace of life. For me, society is an intoxicating party—and perhaps it always will be. But home is home. Solitude is the dwelling that sustains and nurtures me, even in times of felt loneliness.

*   *   *

One day a friend was in my prayer room. She read my covenant and asked, "Where is the vow of celibacy?" It was the first time I saw what seemed to be an obvious omission. The covenant had evolved out of a sense of presence with God. Surely, by implication, the solitary was celibate. Why, then, no vow?

When I recalled the conversation to my spiritual director, a Carmelite nun, she said, "It's implied as a result of all the other vows." In other words, if I lived in solitude and silence, with a life of simplicity, solidarity and obedience, to be in constant prayer—celibacy was the state I would have to live in to attain that lifestyle.

I have, since then, searched the mystical literature in vain, looking for some guidance into our sexuality in a solitary state. The fact that I omitted that vow was, to me, significant. Why?

Celibacy is placed, by the church, on a pedestal. I have now read countless books that say it frees you to love universally. It admits it entails a struggle. It discourages masturbation or self-pleasuring oneself. It advises one to distract oneself when the sexual urge presents itself. In other words, if you wish to pursue a spiritual life, you must apply your will away from your sexual self.

The mystics, by and large, were silent on the subject. However, when a woman or a man entered deeply into the mystical presence of God, inevitably they became celibate—even if married.

The reality is that it is hard to be alone. It goes against instinct. The vow of celibacy can, in fact, mutilate the spiritual journey. It can provide safe haven for the woman, or man, who fears sexual intimacy—and thereby block the ordinary human pathway to love. It can harden the heart with pride and self-righteousness by constantly telling the celibate person, *"You have chosen the harder way, the better way, the more holy way."* It can drive the Spirit of God away like a shrew beating the Divine Lover away with a stick.

Celibacy is a very serious vow.

I never consider myself celibate for more than a day. It is, for now, a way of life that God has given me the *grace* to live in—and if the grace is gone tomorrow, and I am torn to pieces by sexual desire, I *still* consider that to be totally of God.

No vow can heal a schism within the soul. If a person has compartmentalized spiritual energy as "good" and sexual energy as "bad"—the virgin and the whore—no amount of willpower will press it down into extinction. Unresolved, it will become the dark shadow defeating the desire of the soul seeking God.

While the division exists, the solitary has to be willing to go deeper into—not flee from—human neediness. That searching and self-examination often opens strange doors. I have heard all too often—and experienced for myself—the surprise of human love. But how can the solitary, living in solitude, fall in love?

In a modern society, the silent dweller worships with others, often has a job, sees close friends for spiritual nourishment, has a spiritual director, encounters doctors, and other health care professionals on a regular basis. There are numerous opportunities for even the solitary—being quite human—to fall in love.

Human love challenges the perceived call to solitude. It allows it to be strengthened, or it allows it to end. While I have not liked finding myself in love, I do not fight it as contrary to my felt sense of vocation.

I do take my vow of solitude seriously. I know from experience that such a human love, if it touches deeply into my heart, will require years, not months or days, to reach God's will for it over my own. And if solitude is the deeper call, it will mean that love will be transformed into something as subtle as a gentle wind blowing over me.

It is not the *speed* with which we do things, but the *direction* in which we do them. If one finds oneself in love, sitting with the emotion and praying is a steadfast, if slow way through it. If solitude is the stronger call, eventually the relationship must take its rightful place as friendship, or sacred memory. One does not have to rush out of the door of human love for fear of losing God and everything one desires. No. It is better to take time—years if necessary—to clean up the house, psychologically speaking, then say a caring, gentle, good-bye to the dream of human union—and return to your solitude.

*   *   *

Is there such a thing as natural celibacy, a celibacy worn so comfortably that one is oblivious to the sexual pull of love?

While I do not think there is a natural biological state of celibacy, there is grace. The natural celibate is one whose biologically driven sexual loving self and spirit-driven soulful loving self have found inseparable union in one another. It is truly grace, and no one can predict the time or place or way—or even if—such union will occur. A sense of unified equilibrium undergirds one's solitude, but it is an equilibrium that may be unbalanced later.

This may not mean the grace was not ever given, but that the person is being invited to a deeper level of sexual/spiritual integration.

For myself, a key integration occurred once when I felt admired sexually as a woman, and delighted in spiritually as a creation of God. Being held with human love in that mix—and trusting the person who offered it—allowed a transformation to take place within me. Whereas I felt divided before, with a hungry sexual self craving satiation, and a hungry spiritual self seeking union, now there was peace within my body as though union between the two had occurred. Knit and interwoven, I cannot quite conceive of one acting without the other anymore. My spirituality is sexual; my sexuality is spiritual.

It freed me to move more authentically into solitude. The friendship, while dear in my memory, no longer needed the real-time-and-space commitment so contrary to solitude.

Natural celibacy is like a mature loving marriage. Just as in such a marriage, you are not "looking for love," but resting in it, so the celibate rests within the union of self-and-God.

The natural celibate can go deeper into the cave of solitude than would be possible if the sexual self is still in a divided state. When division is there, the solitary will be driven out of the cave by the need to alleviate the anxiety the division itself provokes. When natural celibacy is present, the solitary comes and goes from the cave more in response to God than to self-driven desires.

*　　*　　*

The natural celibate is never asexual. Here I speak personally. There is absolutely no need to ignore sexual impulses that arise from natural biological rhythms, even though they may be less frequent.

Before natural celibacy, the biological urge for orgasm will skyrocket whenever a love attraction is in an active state. To will abstinence from self-pleasure during this time is, in my opinion, counterproductive, because the will stays completely obsessed with the desire. If our authentic desire is for God, we will not be harmed by self-pleasure. It sustains us as we walk toward a deeper, less ego-driven, love.

The cautions are minimal. It is not very useful to try to *stimulate* the desire. The horrible anguish of human loneliness can be aroused even from seeing worthwhile movies, or reading noteworthy books when they evoke that sense of sexual love. That does not mean to avoid them, but to realize that their effect on the solitary can be harder to handle.

On a practical level, the solitary has to learn to balance his or her sexual urge gently within the whole context of their silent lifestyle. Personally, I do not believe in self-denial. I think it is damaging, and I think it hinders the deeper graces awaiting the solitary of an integrated sexual and spiritual self. Perhaps it is my background. I dated; I flirted; I was married. My sexuality is rooted in lived-out intimacy. As such, it holds no terrors for me. It just *is*.

For me, the deeper sense of comfort within my sexual/spiritual self came by plunging into the very bowels of the dilemma. I always feel that God's work is done best when we are not afraid of anything that may result—to trust in our desire for God and our willingness to follow, and offer our heartfelt prayer.

In the sexual issue for the solitary, I believe one must be willing, absolutely, to abandon one's hope for a vocation of solitude. It is only in surrendering *that* that one may ever hope to emerge as a true solitary. It is not by amputating our sexual nature, it is by going through the fires of passion and confusion of it that we find the deeper truth about our sexual-spiritual nature.

*   *   *

In the end, what my spiritual director said is true. The vocation makes one celibate and not the reverse. If your call truly is to a solitary lifestyle, eventually celibacy must follow. Solitude invites the presence of God, a presence that so consumes the soul, there is no love energy available for an intense human commitment to intimacy.

The deeper one goes into this spiritual solitude, the lighter one travels. But it is not for us to divest ourselves—at our own willed choosing—of the things that are necessary for life within society. It is for God to strip us, often painfully, of them at a time when God knows—if we do not—that we must go more lightly into this Heart of Love.

Simplicity

To Choose to Give Rather Than Receive

Simplicity is not equal with silence, solitude, or prayer, but it will affect it like a light casting its brilliance into a dark room so one can see more clearly. Contrariwise, silence, solitude, and prayer gradually reveal the true meaning of simplicity. It is like the seed that produces the tree that in turn produces the fruit that bears the seed. For that reason, it is a very difficult vow to comprehend, much less live.

In my covenant, not knowing these things, I used the only definition I knew—it was better to give than to receive, to live marginally, and give all the rest to others.

I had a very romantic notion about hermits. They never, or rarely, saw a human being.

How much money did you need to be that kind of a solitary? Not much.

We all have idealized, even romantic, ideas of a hermit. Mine had a self-denying, Thoreau-like quality: a rustic cabin with wood furniture. A single bed. A chair. A table. Hand-carved spoons. One pot, one pan, one glass, one plate. In my mind's eye, it was Shaker-like simplicity that illumined my hunger for unbroken solitude. I enshrined that vision beneath the vow of simplicity. I would not truly be a solitary until I had divested myself of virtually all material possessions.

Until this century, simplicity was the material reality of most people. Without autos, airplanes, phones, radios, television, or computers, our ancestors worked hard but at a simple, biologically human pace. No task could be done faster than seconds strung together by manual labor. There was no such thing as the nanosecond.

Simplicity—even as late as Thoreau's time—was in part the inevitable result of a far simpler society. Unless one was extremely wealthy, the dishes were washed by hand, the clothes wrung through a wringer, the trees chopped by an axe, and bread kneaded by hand. Simplicity occurred when the task—and time—were interwoven harmoniously.

We get an interior sense of such simplicity when the task we are working on matches the inner rhythm of our body. It is like a dance, a waltz, where movement slowly attains an end. It is what the Buddhists call "mindfulness." Building a stone wall, hoeing a garden, washing dishes, even reading, can be rushed through or savored. Too slow and simplicity becomes irritating, boring, monotonous; too fast and simplicity gives way to anxiety as one worries about the next task, or self-glorification over conquering the task so quickly.

The profoundly difficult dilemma for the silent dweller today is to find that rhythm of simplicity in an extraordinarily complex society that sees time as a compressible commodity, and the nanosecond as the new measure of human time.

It is easy for those hungering for solitude to equate the lure of a machineless Luddite society with holy simplicity. It can seem that silence, solitude, and prayer will flourish only in a world devoid of mouse-fetched E-mail, automatic bread-making machines, and electronically monitored automobiles.

There is a seductive attractiveness to primitive simplicity. Just reading the sayings of the Desert Fathers is enough to trigger a simplicity neurosis among any man or woman desiring a solitary lifestyle.

I can speak so well of this because I sought the austerely simple world with dogged determination. Yet I also wanted the beauty of paintings, gentle, quiet furnishings, gardens and plants. Without them, I could not have entered the silent, solitary world for which I hungered. A hermit's hut, stark and barren and seemingly close to God, would have terrified me as much as a prison sentence of solitary confinement.

This knowledge, however, was excruciatingly slow in coming.

Rather than follow God into solitude, I stepped in front of God—machete-swinging my way through a complex world, hewing a simple life in the midst of the vast, complicated infrastructure known as modern society.

Part of the problem was that I had the money to "create" a simple life. Rather than being destitute, I was adequately well off. There was no likelihood that I would ever live in one rented room, or survive on food stamps. I had the luxury of creating a solitary lifestyle, and I was continually haunted by the words of Jesus to the rich man, "Go and sell all you have, and follow me."

But not haunted enough to try. Instinctively I knew I did not have that kind of holy brazenness. Like diving into an icy cold lake, my wobbly sense of vocation would have frozen and drowned.

*   *   *

I began my solitary journey in an apartment. It was my first home after marriage. Out the sliding glass windows I gazed upon undeveloped acreage—a weed-ridden field—and delighted in its unmanicured beauty. But I never felt the apartment was a hermitage. When I began to hunger for a deeper solitude than a shared parking lot and a community pool, I decided to buy a home.

A nearby neighborhood had small brick Cape Cod houses with tiny yards. I drove through the community, thinking to myself, *These houses are the right size for a hermitage.* I actually thought owning my own dwelling place would be cheaper in the long run, thus honoring my vow of simplicity. I soon learned otherwise.

When one went on the market, I asked the realtor if I could be alone in the house. I wanted to know if it had the right feel for someone who would want to live in solitude. She agreed and I spent one morning quietly standing, sitting, walking through the empty rooms. The sun came through the front windows. I watched dust motes like microscopic solitaries float through the house.

This, I felt in the deep center of my hunger, was my hermitage.

I signed the papers, parted with the money, and took the keys off the settlement table.

I soon found that the only discordant note to my dream of owning a hermitage was how much my expression of solitude would eventually *cost*. I could perhaps whittle away at my personal possessions; I could gradually lower my standard of living, but I couldn't lower taxes or insurance premiums. If I wanted to live within the security net that modern society provided, my suburban simplicity would have a huge price tag.

There was the cost of a house in the suburbs—no small expense—plus completely furnishing three floors, plus numerous repairs required to upgrade the utilities. Because I thought it would be my "forever hermitage," I spared nothing. Dollars poured out into the hands of carpenters, plumbers, electricians, and handymen.

As I slowly saw its beauty unfold, I fell more deeply in love with its sheltering silence. I also anguished over the bills. Increasingly, I pitted my interpretation of simplicity against the cost of creating an environment for solitude, and could not reconcile the two. I felt selfish and indulgent—a make-believe "hermit" who suffered no discomfort. It just destroyed any sense of gratitude I had for the house, or to God for providing me with secure shelter.

I called it the Taj Mahal hermitage.

I was anxious all the time, having one foot, psychologically, in my hermitage, and the other roving around looking for the *ideal* hermit dwelling. Occasionally, I wondered if perhaps God *needed* a silent dweller in the suburbs, but those thoughts were like the flutter of a bird's wings across my anxious mind.

It wasn't until I added the last bauble that I realized I could never *build* solitude, simple or not. Fear of solitude made me overprotect myself. Solitude was too lonely, prayer too vulnerable, silence too naked. If I could adorn this seeming vocation with beauty and peaceful security, perhaps I would not be afraid of what I most wanted.

I feared absolute aloneness with God and sought to comfort myself with possessions. I would create a beautiful three-dimensional artistic statement of solitude, and bypass the reality of it.

I knew, instinctively and from experience, that the real battles—with loneliness, rejection, anger, depression, boredom, and even the relentless impact of solitude itself—still remained ahead.

It seems that Thomas Merton, Trappist monk and prolific writer on the spiritual life, was also wooed by the lure of the Desert Fathers. Throughout his monastic life, he longed to live as a hermit. Stymied by his superior, he spent decades in community life before he attained his desire. Eventually he received permission to live in a cinder-block dwelling, a simple structure, in the woods of the Gesthemane Abbey in Kentucky. It was to be the setting for his hermit solitude to unfold. A hermit's hut— a poor man's dwelling.

For whatever reason, shortly after he was established within his longed-for solitude, he told his friends how they could slip into the monastery grounds by a back way, thereby gaining access to him in his hermitage. And they told their friends, and thus he destroyed the idealized solitude he had so insistently fought for within his community. Simplicity, concretized in cinder blocks, had not removed the real obstacles to communion with God.

It is very hard to be an *idealized* hermit. It is much more realistic to be an ordinary one. I am sure Merton sometimes laughed at his own folly. He was the sociable hermit who loved his guests almost as much as he loved his solitude.

One day I was quietly sitting in prayer once again lamenting my inability to *acquire* the simple lifestyle I felt essential to the solitary. I felt a demanding voice within me saying, *Stop. Just stop.* Stop trying. Stop creating. Stop evading. Simply *be*. Be human. Be vulnerable. Be a failure. *That* is simplicity.

It was too simple for me to comprehend. Like the artist rejecting her painting as having too many strokes, I began to search for another hermitage.

I decided to sell the house I had lavished so much love on, and buy or build a much smaller, more primitive, house in a rural setting. I would be more isolated, and have an even more unrelentingly solitary lifestyle, at one-quarter the cost of my suburban setting. I was *sure* that with material simplicity—akin to Merton's cinder block dwelling—my inner vision of myself as a silent dweller would match my outer reality.

I looked at forested property with views. Land with streams running through it. Tiny farms nestled in rolling mountains. I wanted each one. Yet whenever I consulted my silent interior, I was always told, "No." The steadfast force that had guided me throughout my spiritual journey was like a compass always pointing home.

My quest for simplicity was the burr that stuck in my solitary saddle. I could not live with it, nor could I dislodge it no matter how much it irritated my rigid definitions.

It was during this time that I had two dreams.

In the first, an inner city bishop was in my prayer room polishing a round wood table. He seemed quietly filled with deep joy and peace. Meanwhile, I was on my hands and knees across the hall in another room picking up shiny copper pennies and dead pine needles. I looked over at him and felt deeply, *I am supposed to be there, not here.*

In the next dream, I was polishing the exposed white roots of a tree. They stood so high I could walk right through them without bending. I felt the same joy the bishop had in polishing the table. The roots were silky smooth to the touch.

I could not understand the meaning of those dreams.

I kept looking for the ideal hermitage. One day I signed a contract for a run-down farmhouse on the edge of a small town in western Maryland. My sister was appalled by what she saw. The house had dry rot in the eaves, the floor sloped, the fifty-year-old linoleum buckled and peeled, the toilet wouldn't flush, the septic system seeped sewage down the side of the road, and there was minimal insulation. The wind howled through the house. Only the hardy could withstand the mountainously cold winter.

But I loved the view. The field of buckwheat across the road, the mountains in the background, the twenty-minute walk to the small town, the old stone church, the cozy library, friendly post office, and cheap diner. It was my solitary dream.

To my sister's relief, the contract fell through. Well acquainted with my stubbornness, she looked for another solution to my insistence on finding solitude in the simple primitive setting. She suggested an RV. "Then when you need to live this simple life alone in nature," she argued, "you can take your hermitage with you."

One day I visited an RV show out of curiosity, and soon I was wheeling a twenty-two-foot five-ton Coachman around. In a moment of solitary insanity, I now owned *two* hermitages—all in pursuit of *simplicity.*

I left my Taj Mahal hermitage and began to tour the U.S. in my hermitage-on-wheels. For the next year, I was home sporadically. The grass died. The vegetables withered. The house, often used by other guests, became "rearranged."

I was finally living in a one-room cabin, albeit with a stuffed fold-out cushy sofa, a built-in microwave, retractable rotating TV antenna, queen-sized bed, and full refrigerator.

I sat in state parks, national parks, local parks, KOA campgrounds, private campgrounds, and friend's driveways, tied to an umbilical electric cord snaking out one side. I looked at incredible beauty; I sat in splendid isolation; I mimicked twenty-two by eight foot simplicity. And I thought, *I can live like this. This is all I need.*

Ignoring my prayerful insights, I felt I had finally experienced simplicity. I could sell the house, live far more cheaply in an RV, and follow the weather patterns.

But I had no roots.

I came home exhausted from fighting my way through snow and ice on my final trek across the country in late October. I unlocked the door to my home and pushed it open. Stunned by its quiet unassuming beauty, I felt an aching cry within me.

I now understood the dreams.

*   *   *

Trying to scoop up copper pennies was my attempt to reduce my understanding of the vow of simplicity to the single dimension of money. And not even nickels or dimes or quarters, but shiny pennies. I had idealized poverty, and was idolatrizing the perfect symbol of it—a copper penny. I had no time for silence, solitude, and prayer; I was caught, frustrated and anxious, in the inconsequential, time-consuming task of honoring my rigid and unforgiving definition of simplicity. But as I looked up, I could see the bishop, in quiet simple motions polishing the table in my prayer room. Love, joy, and gratitude seemed to radiate out of his body. What I saw before me was the pure simplicity of a soul delighting in God.

While he worked on the table, I gathered up dead pine needles. True simplicity, I believed, could only be found in the primitiveness of untamed nature. Without it, my desire for solitude would dry up and die, slowly suffocated by modern society. I could not be a solitary unless I had the perfect setting. But now, I wondered if it was really my dead-needled insistence on defining a simple hermit's life my own way that stood in the way of soulful communion with God.

And what of the polished bone-white roots of the tree?

They were my hermitage. I moved in and out of their sheltering arms, always staying close, as I slowly warmed them with the touch of my hands. Lost in the timeless motion, I smoothed them to silken touch. It was here, doing this, I felt at home. The hermitage, I at last understood, is where the soul becomes simple before God.

*   *   *

Simplicity, I have learned, is the gradual reconciliation between the outer world and the inner one. A sign of disharmony occurs when there is an excess on either side. The simplicity God wanted from me was not material simplicity but spiritual simplicity—spiritual dependence and trust.

I am at last attached to my dwelling. There *is* a material simplicity that slowly comes to the silent dweller. It cannot be forced or hurried. It is the work of solitude, silence, and prayer. As they become the priceless treasures for the hermit, material needs slowly become less important. For me, this change is not a steady thing, but one that moves forward and backward, as though circling in a sinuous curve deeper and deeper into the Unknown. There is no hurry, and no need to reach a destination.

I notice other small things about simplicity.

The house often tells me. While my work is writing, I find that unless the house is at rest and in order, my sense of silence, solitude, and prayer is wounded. It is more important for me to tend to the house, to nurture it back to quiet stillfulness, than to write. I stop to pick things up, to clean, and increasingly often, to give away something that once seemed essential to my solitude.

Silence, solitude, and prayer also bring another dimension of simplicity into clearer focus. The pace of life becomes simpler. Spiritual simplicity seems to call for attentiveness to the task at hand. It is not so much the task itself that engages one's energies as it is an inner quieting concentration—a simple single-mindedness. When I write, or clean, or walk the dog, it is easier to enjoy that one task. I think we were made for joy, and often we forego that joy by thinking ahead of or behind our moment. Often the problem arises because we think too many things are essential to our life when in fact very few are.

I am, by nature, slow. Either I do many things without joy, or a few things with joy. That is my pace. I love to read. It is my passion. But I read very slowly. One to two books a month. I could learn to speed read. I could push myself harder and faster. But joy would vanish. I would have more knowledge, but little joy.

The simple life appears to be one lived deliberately. Thoreau said he did not want to die without having known the depth and breadth of a human life not wasted.

I often think of how I felt within the dream when I polished the bone-white roots of the dead tree. There was no hurry. Each stroke itself contained all knowledge, all mystery, all joy, all gratitude. The roots were worn smooth by love and caring attention. The tree was not dead—no more than the cross Jesus died on is dead. The tree was willing to reveal all of itself, even its roots, for my sake. To allow me to touch and love and polish it—just as Jesus allowed us to touch all of him.

That is the holy core of simplicity. Of our own merits, we are like seeds throwing ourselves on rocky paths. The path seems sure and straight, but the seed cannot gain a foothold in such soil. Yet when we stop and trust the wind of our desire to scatter and blow us onto the soil of holy simplicity, then we can take root and grow. We become a tree rooted in unknowable simplicity that illumines God. And eventually, we bear fruit with hidden seed to be sown in the modern world.

Solidarity

To Choose Oneness with the Poor and Dispossessed by Becoming Poor and Dispossessed

Aloneness carries with it a certain poverty. While time alone brings a deep richness, prolonged aloneness results in a certain loss.

The need to be alone is part of the human condition. Every person, no matter how extroverted his or her lifestyle, needs time to pause, to reflect, to simply rest in soulful silence. But for the silent dweller, choosing solidarity with one's own human aloneness is a particular form of poverty and deprivation. Family, spouse, children, religious community, volunteer work, professional work—all of these add the essential ingredient of companionship to one's life. These are absent when one chooses a life of deliberate solitude.

Of the five vows, this one continues to be the most enigmatic to me. What link did I sense between solidarity with the poor and a deliberate solitary lifestyle?

When I included solidarity in my covenant, it was not because I had a clear understanding of it. I repeatedly asked both myself and God, *Why is this here?* Other than an almost adamant sense that it remain, I received no answer. It became the "shadow vow"—the one I could not live out because I did not know how to live it out.

Now, five years later, I am beginning to understand that truly healthy solitude requires a groundedness in the human condition. This vow is slowly becoming a ballast to the romanticism that has surrounded my desire to be solitary.

*   *   *

Some years ago, I had a dream. In it, I was on a mountain trail. A man intercepted me and placed a dying older woman at my feet. I carried her to the valley. When I laid her down, her coat fell open and a tightly held sheaf of papers became visible. She clutched them to her chest with dying fingers. When I pried the papers from her, they looked like a doctoral dissertation, with many hand-written corrections.

The dream remained an enigma for a long time, but I kept being drawn to the woman. She mirrored a great deal of myself—my love of knowledge and wanting to possess it. Obviously, she was seeking spiritual knowledge for she had been found high on the mountain—too high to live. And there was a tenacity about her—a willingness to die if need be—to obtain this knowledge, to complete this quest.

Yet somehow, it had all gone wrong. She was killing herself with her obsession to *know* God. And she was, in a sense, almost destroyed by her greed. She collapsed from physical exhaustion, and had to be removed from her heights. It was unclear whether she would live or die when the dream ended.

One day I asked what was the proper way for a woman to dwell on the spiritual mountain. And immediately I saw a woman who also held a sheaf of papers, unbound. But the writing on it was indecipherable. It was embossed with the invisibleness of God. She had so many pages in her hand that the source of them seemed infinite, and endlessly plentiful.

She had a graciousness, a gentleness, about her. And she seemed to be giving praise to God. Not the praise of words or specific prayers—but her whole being was one adoration, one continual union with love pouring out into the heavens. Yet she was not unaware of earth and what was beneath her. To the contrary, it was for this that she sang. She was well aware of the pain and the sorrow, the injustice and cruelty, the poor and the destitute, the rich and the unhappy. She had deep compassion—far more than what one human could contain.

Like a mother, she saw each one of us. What we felt—our joy, sorrow, laughter, pain—was like a membrane wrapped around her heart. She did not sing with word or with sound, but with *being*. Her love for God poured *through* this human membrane to God in total and absolute abandon, in total adoration.

Because of this dream, I can feel within myself two types of solidarity—two completely different stories. One is comprehensible on human terms; the other incomprehensible.

*   *   *

Before I entered a more solitary lifestyle, I traveled to El Salvador three times to visit our sister parish in earthquake-torn San Salvador. Their economic poverty was enormous. Sewage ran down the road; shacks were built on garbage dumps. Yet on Sunday morning, I would see little girls emerge from these hovels dressed in clean dresses with white socks, and shiny shoes, their hair combed and tied with barrettes and ribbons. Such a scene made poverty an enigma to me.

I spent one day with a mother, a tortilla maker who had seven children. She boiled field corn in a tin washtub, carried it on her head to the community spigot, washed and cooled it, took it to the local grinder and ground it. Then she cooked the corn dough into tortillas on a fire-heated sheet of dry metal in a hot tin shed, and sold each one for two cents.

At the end of the day, I was nauseous from the heat. She purchased a cold soft drink to cool me. Before I left, I gave her a small bag of trail mix—cashews, raisins, almonds, pineapple — something you cannot buy in El Salvador. I expected her to hoard it for her family. But she opened the bag, gave a few pieces to each of her children, and began to walk through her entire village, sharing with each person she met.

Her immediate empathy—and solidarity with—her impoverished community has remained my most vivid image of what it means to be one with the poor. Hers was an active outward sign of equality and justice. She received a treasure; she shared it.

Somehow I have instinctively always known that without human solidarity, human solitude would be a fraud. But the inner integrity of that solidarity—within a solitary lifestyle—has remained elusive, mysterious, and enigmatic.

*　　*　　*

If deepest humanity is writ upon the *soul*, then the solitary—in communing so deeply with soul and spirit—lives out a deep expression of that humanity. It is in letting go of all that seems to be human—companionship, human love, service, children— that one begins to touch the unseen roots that feed society and make it grow and thrive.

But this letting go is not abandoning, or turning one's back on humanity. It is letting go of the *way* such connections are held within the human heart.

The mountain woman in my dream who clutched at God, determined to be one with God in her knowing is like the rich man who thinks he can buy solidarity with the poor by writing large checks to charity. Because that dream is mine, there is a part of me—a significant part—that believes I can own God. I nurture this illusion of my poverty by going up on the mountain of human isolation—depriving myself of companionship—and equate this journey to "oneness with the poor and dispossessed."

It is the dark side of this vow of solidarity. It has no life. It can only result in bitterness, human isolation, and psychological death.

The journey into authentic solidarity is a very difficult journey that I am only beginning to understand. True solidarity requires a profound sense of inner integration into the pain and horror—and awe and beauty—of being human.

I have read so many books about the holiness of *aloneness*, and the psychological neediness of *loneliness*. For me, both run together in a river. I am alone—and lonely—in the same indrawn breath. I feel the awe and holiness of my aloneness; I feel the sharp wounding pain of my loneliness. The two become so one that it is impossible for me to say, like coffee and creamy sugar, what part is bitter, and what the sweet milk?

The first step toward true solidarity is accepting our human poverty. It is hard to keep one's heart open to the enormity of one's pain—and not rush back to human consolation. And why? Why *not* run to our brothers and sisters? We are meant to be human, to be in communion. What strange disorder possesses the solitary to seek a solidarity that cannot be seen, touched, or affirmed?

*   *   *

Though I did not know it when I joined the adult world filled with images of myself as successful, married, and independent, I was not living a human life. I was living a socially acceptable life, one complex construction of endless illusion and delusion. I was living in the acute deprivation of soul. I was truly poor and dispossessed of the authentic humanness to which each one of us is invited.

I was in the dark, and did not know it, and did not know how to find the light.

Yet it is in precisely that kind of darkness that true Light—the light of a Spirit-lit soul—can finally emerge from its own delusion. It is as though all of us are like lighthouses, beacons of intense illuminating Light—but we do not know how to turn our soul-light on. We don't know how to cast out life-saving illumination into the world. We are poor and we do not know how to become rich. We don't know how to be in solidarity with anyone—poor and dispossessed or not—because we do not yet know how to be in solidarity with our own human soul.

To learn such a thing, we must go into the dark unlit lighthouse—and wait. Such lighthouses of the soul do not speak. They are listened to in the deepest darkest silence of night. And in the meantime, during the day, one does the chores.

I wish I could find the words to share my own struggle.

It is like waiting. Like being at a deserted bus stop on a dark night in a town where all are asleep in their houses. And not knowing if buses really stop at this corner. Being told by one person—a stranger—to stand here. Standing, waiting, sitting, as day passes to night and the streets slowly empty, and the shops close, and husbands go home to wives, and wives to husbands, and children go to bed. You see light shining out of windows, and still you stand sentinel on the empty corner. One by one, the lights go out. The people are there, but they are not there. And still you wait.

That is the hopeless trust the solitary places in listening for the Light that will illumine our soul and make us one with our incarnation. And listening is the right word, for this Light is not seen by eyes nor comprehended by the mind, but only heard in the utter silence of the soul.

Perhaps a whole lifetime of such listening is not enough. Perhaps one day *is* enough. But we all go, at times in our life, to the lighthouse within—across the rough dark waters of our fear, away from humankind, alone, unprotected, afraid of dying, afraid of living.

At this point in our journey, we cannot even conceive of singing adorations to God through the membrane of humanity surrounding our heart.

*   *   *

I have always felt the longing to touch—and be touched—by love, human love. To be vulnerable to it, to immerse myself in it. And I have, more than once, allowed such love into the deepest part of my soul. In those moments, I am no longer alone or lonely, but part of *love*—the universal force that binds all of creation together and stretches its wings far past life and death.

Why—when I can experience such glorious human union— do I yet hunger for *solitude*? Am I arrogantly standing outside the human condition—like the mountain woman clutching her written understandings—as though refusing to be immersed in the balm of human companionship? Do I want to be God? Do I have some misplaced need to be different, exotic, apart from my own humanity?

Well, it would not surprise me.

The longer I stay in this solitude, the lighthouse beacon casts a harsh life-giving glare over my own neediness—for recognition, for having some value in this life, for being loved. Worse, I wonder *if this is even the path I am to be on, or if it is romantic delusion?*

I am between the utterly human mountain woman who judges her merit by the tenaciousness of her grasp upon God, and the open-handed silent woman who holds countless pages of love and sings through the human condition to God.

To let go of the mountain woman within me, I find myself walking, with great trepidation, directly into the neurotic jungle of my greatest *fear.* Of being poor and dispossessed. Of being utterly forgotten and of no worth in the kingdom of God.

Fear seduces the solitary to abandon her quest. Within me, I often feel horrible debilitating uselessness. During those times— and they are horrible—I feel utter emotional helplessness.

Ironically, I really *do not* want to be one with the poor and dispossessed. I am terrified of such a possibility because to me it means a kind of human oblivion, a negation of the human spirit. Yet it is in precisely that poverty that the core essence of our human solidarity with one another becomes manifest.

Out of the junk and debris of our emotional trash comes the child dressed in beauty. And that child knows how to sing through the human condition to God.

*   *   *

We live in an increasingly illusory world, one where images define our response to life. This is the true poverty we live in today. It is so enmeshed in our culture and our life, it is virtually impossible to distinguish it from the true humanity we are called to embrace, one honoring the soul, and rich in authentic love and commitment.

Those who deliberately choose solitude are not posturing as holy people. They are simply trying to recapture true humanity in an increasingly image-driven world. They sense a fraud—like hearing canned laughter during a sitcom when nothing is funny—and know no other way to confront it than simply to depart, for a while.

Some of us enter solitude to ferret out our illusions. We sense we are entrapped by them, and step apart to see how their subtle tentacles strangle our authentic life story. Such a solitary will be called back into active human community. Theirs is a "vision quest"—a search for clarity—for their soul's journey.

If we go inward on a vision quest, we will probably take a taste of this poverty back with us into the world. But we will not *be* poor until we stay and become one with our own poverty.

The solitary agrees to live within the world and universe *of his or her own body*—for a time. It contains everything—human truth, and horrible lie. The silent dweller listens inwardly to the story he or she has constructed, using the illusions at hand. What seemed real and valid in a high-tech, media-driven world becomes, when deprived of the artificial glow of those neon-lighted expectations, inhuman and unreal.

We pass through our own illusory world where even our "goodness" covers a poverty of neediness and loneliness, a hunger for approval and acceptance, power and fame, beauty and fortune. The longer we stay in solitude, the more silence impregnates us with the radiant light of human truth. We become, in some strange way, married to our humanness.

The vow of solidarity, which seems almost marginal to the substance of my covenant, may in fact be the very heart of it. It is *the* link between the utter aloneness of the human condition—and its utter communion with humanity.

The woman who sings her adoration to God *through* the human condition, is the embodiment of solidarity. In her, God and the world are inseparable. Her soundless joy is the lighthouse. In her, I somehow dimly perceive the solitary is in solidarity with the human condition, which is poor and dispossessed of the inexhaustible richness of God.

Obedience

To Honor the Obligations of My Life
over My Own Preferences

Obedience has always perplexed me. Being brought up by an atheist father, I had no childhood concept of obedience to God. It never occurred to me that I was "good" or "bad" if I followed—or did not follow—church doctrine or discipline. Later, when I joined the Roman Catholic Church, I learned the weight of attaining salvation. Volumes of canon law, centuries of church teachings, and daily guidance from priests presumed to protect me and my fragile new faith. Belief in Christ had erupted like a hidden artesian well within me; faith-lived-out, I would soon learn, was hemmed in by a long tradition of obedience.

Solitude has its dangers. The romantic idea of being alone with God, and the reality of finding yourself with your *self* in utter aloneness can be too stark, too frightening, a landscape. Depression, anxiety, doubt, even anger, are part of the journey in learning to be alone with God.

Obedience, properly defined, can be a source of consolation and security in the seemingly boundarylessness of endless silence and solitude. It can ground the solitary in secure soil, and serve as a necessary nutrient to its healthy growth.

No external recognized criteria exist within the Church today to guide the solitary with regard to obedience. The Church has devoted its full attention to issues of obedience within the *physical community* of believers, whether lay or monastic. Being a corporate expression of faith, the Church has no basis upon which to prescribe obedience for noncorporate experiences of solitude. The definitions for obedience, therefore, must come from within and from the solitude itself.

The purpose of the solitary is to gaze upon God with as little blinking as possible. God yearns to be known by us, yet as a people, we fear to know God. We busy ourselves; we describe love but are terrified to be held in its unrelenting embrace. We prefer to write theologies and infallible teachings than admit we know no more about the Divine than when we were a child.

The solitary anchors the active Christian community. The community is like the crew of a ship sailing under Christ. The anchor lies as ballast in the hold. It steadies the ship with weighted silence. Occasionally, the anchor is tossed overboard to secure the ship. It sinks into deep unknowing, holding in some mysterious way the ship in safety.

Another way of imaging the solitary as a unique member of the Christian community comes from Paul's image—we are all parts of one body. I once asked myself, *What part of the body of Christ am I?* Mentally, I imaged the different parts of this body and was surprised to find that I fit nowhere. I was not eye nor hands, feet nor heart. It was then that I realized I had passed by, as irrelevant, the soles of the feet.

The solitary is the sole of the Body of Christ. Entirely hidden, but carrying the weight of the body. When the sun is directly overhead, when the body is closest to God's love, the solitary is most hidden, casting not even a shadow.

Or, the hermit is like Jonah, swallowed into the whale of love that is God. The solitary lives in the stomach of God. It is so frightening that I have often hoped God would spit me out onto the shore of the life I wanted.

What makes the solitary so difficult for the Church to comprehend is that what is happening cannot be seen. We do not know what happened to John the Baptist or St. Paul in the desert. There is an impenetrable veil of silence over those years and times. Yet we are drawn to their desert experiences because they returned carrying a light within themselves that we carry only faintly. It burned uncovered in our midst.

The hermit simply illumines, and lives out, the call to prayer. It is a mystery not even the solitary understands, and many people have misconceptions about solitude.

Thomas Merton, who had the hermit's desire, confounded people by his excessive joy in being with others. There is this assumption that hermits must be outwardly what they desire inwardly. But Merton drank in deeply those moments of communal love so that he could continue his journey into the vast emptiness of God.

*   *   *

The problem for today's lay solitary is that there is no rule, no monastic superior to obey. True, the hermit should be under spiritual direction, but it is unlikely that today's spiritual director will dictate how solitude should be lived. First, the spiritual director very likely is within a communal setting, and probably has no firsthand experience of the kind of solitude the hermit seeks. Second, there is a maturing in spiritual direction today that trusts in the Holy Spirit. Often the director simply listens with a deeply prayerful presence to see if it is God working in the individual, or not. I had one director who, after I poured my heart out for an hour, simply said, "God is working in you."

Then she picked up her calendar to set the next date. I was upset with her. I wanted orders to *obey* so that I could climb the spiritual ladder. Instead she, and my directors since then, left me to the silent, nontangible presence of God.

So, the vow of obedience cannot, for the lay solitary, mean obeying a church authority figure. And rarely if ever does God intervene in one's life with such clarity that one is absolutely certain he or she is obeying or disobeying God.

So the solitary has the intense discomfort of having no orders to obey, no superior to follow, and only a vague sense of direction from God.

There are degrees of solitude, but the important point—from the perspective of the Church—is what transpires in solitude. While Jesus, and St. Paul, and the prophets, lived for lengthy times in solitude, they always rejoined the community of believers and fully participated in communal life.

The Church questions: is this call to solitude of God, or is it an unhealthy form of messiah egotism? The solitary will soon learn that the Church views this vocation with extreme caution. A healthy sign that the call is authentic is that the solitary herself views the call with skepticism. By committing myself to be obedient to the obligations of my life over my own preferences, I was basically saying to God, "I accept solitude—with the door wide open back into my community."

The vow of obedience, in a way, serves as a safety valve. It means simply to honor the obligations of one's life. We are not hatched, newborn, into solitude. We have come from somewhere—some prior societal life with friends, family, and obligations.

As we disentangle and disengage, there is still a residual core of obligations that are "ours" and no one else's. It may be an aging parent, a neighbor whom we have befriended, a son or daughter, even a spouse. If God is calling you into solitude, your relationships to those whom you have loved may change in the *way* it is lived out—but not the value of it.

As I slowly disentangled myself from a family lifestyle, the vow of obedience became the portal between the two—solitude and society. I had a mother's responsibility to my children. Also, my mother began to suffer the first signs of Alzheimer's—and I was the daughter closest and most available to be her primary decision maker. I would spend considerable time with her as she made several lifestyle changes, and as I gradually took over her affairs.

Then there were the friends who, while they could not comprehend a call to solitude, were willing to struggle along with me to find new terms of relationship.

So, while I hungered for solitude, I had an entire complex of obligations that tied me securely to society. Other solitaries I know are single, but must work for a living. Solitude is not a clean-cut affair.

A part of me simply wanted to go—to begin, in an absolute way, this call to solitude I found so compelling. But the vow of obedience, which I instinctively included in my covenant, kept my feet firmly anchored in the messiness of real life.

Obedience, then, comes from responding to—not initiating—the circumstances of one's life. If my daughter wants me to go shopping with her in the mall, I say yes. If my mother's prescriptions need to be refilled, I go. If a friend calls and needs to talk for an hour, I listen. I stop what I am doing and devote myself to the other person. But I don't call others because my calendar is empty, or I am bored, or because I feel guilty because I am not volunteering.

Responding to the obligations of my life puts solid ground under the vow of obedience. It entails a certain amount of suffering. I might be reading or praying or meditating when the interruption comes. It may require that I immediately stop what I am doing and attend to this need—even when I feel inadequate, unqualified, or somehow unable to do it.

Beneath every vocational call is *love*. If I am called to be a hermit, I am called so that God can open me up completely to compassion for others. As one priest says, "When we meet God, we will not be asked about our gifts. We will be asked how we treated our family."

As solitude matures, a gentle flowing sense of love begins to ripple out, seemingly in all directions. To allow and nurture that is the gift of the solitary within the Christian community.

Being obedient to the obligations of one's life, however, does not mean that every intrusion must be honored. Telephone solicitations, invitations to go out and have a beer, suggestions that you might enjoy meeting a person as a potential mate— these are some obvious examples of intrusions that can be turned down.

With friends, the area can easily become gray. I stay connected with three circles of friends who meet for spiritual sharing. Even though none of them are solitaries, I find their love of God, shared in a *quiet, intimate* setting, is a food I need and must eat in order to maintain healthy solitude.

Throughout the journey into solitude, both for the beginner and the more experienced, I think we face periods where we *want* intrusions, so in very little ways we let others know we are "available." Of course, Merton provides the funniest example by opening the back gate as he is closing the front gate to his hermitage.

Rather than responding to requests, we begin to initiate. A friend calls and we enjoy talking so much that we end the conversation with, "Call whenever you want. I love talking to you," rather than, "Take good care of yourself, now." One initiates; the other stays within the limits of responding only. With time, the solitary can spot the subtle and often funny solitude-escaping tendencies he or she invents.

But core obligations always override solitude. The hermit leaves the hermitage, *hoping* to come back. If a need arises for my children, my mother, my sister, or a close friend, it overrides any desire I have for solitude. I have a variety of ways in which I can respond, some far more suitable to the hermit than others, but respond I must.

*   *   *

As my call to solitude became clearer, a dilemma arose that required that I make a very painful choice. My deepening sense of obedience forced me to forgo one of the greatest comforts I received as a member of the Catholic community—participation in daily Eucharist.

Initially, I incorporated daily Mass into my solitary routine. I began the day in contemplation—a silent sitting with God. At seven, I left for a nearby parish for Mass. Then I returned, and began my solitary day.

I wanted and needed the comfort of community as I faced the sometimes frightening prospects of a solitary lifestyle. However, as the solitude deepened, I found it harder and harder to break off prayer to leave in time for Mass. The early morning hours drew me deeply into contemplation. I slowly began to realize I could not be in two places at one time: in solitude and in community.

The Church opens the day with daily Mass and Eucharist just as the solitary opens hers with solitary contemplation and prayer—responding to the same divine rhythm. Dawn and dusk have always been the portal for God and humanity. The ancient rhythms of the Church, through liturgical expression, open the day with psalms, prayer, and Eucharist. For religious communities, they are one fabric interwoven in a common site. For the laity in active ministry throughout the world, Eucharist provides a bridge between home and the communality of the workplace. They must leave one for the other; the Eucharistic moment of morning Mass provides the bridge.

For the hermit, however, responding to that mystical rhythm requires solitude. I rest and move slowly during those times. I feed in the dawn and the dusk of the day. God's presence is like morning dew. And when that dew has evaporated, so too has daily Mass ended.

*   *   *

All solitaries are different and their response to solitude is unique. I tried for a long time to incorporate solitude and daily Eucharist into my life. But as the solitude deepened, I felt I was ripping the very fabric God was weaving within me every time I put on my coat, got my car keys, drove through rush-hour traffic, and entered into a vibrant community where conversation was expected. Eventually I simply could not leave the presence of God to travel to the presence of God-in-community. A great sadness came over me, and a hunger to be fed by my community—to be recognized as a valid part of the Body of Christ doing God's work.

I looked for images to ease the pain. I remembered when, as a candidate seeking confirmation in the Catholic Church, I could not receive the Eucharist no matter how much I hungered for it or how deep was my understanding of the Last Supper. Obedience required that I abstain. This can be considered a cruel punishment, one that Jesus himself would never inflict on his disciples—or it can be considered total grace.

It was very difficult. I understood fully that this food was the food I wanted, was the very food I most hungered for—yet the Church would not give it to me. I watched, day by day, as others ate the food I wanted.

But slowly, I came to understand that I was the child being nursed by the Church. The Christian community ate for me; the food was digested by their acts; and I received the purest form of Eucharist that was possible—the milk from the breast of the community of believers. I was suckled with a finer food, one that was truly incarnate, between God and human. Obedience in this situation allowed me to reach a profoundly deeper understanding of community.

I wanted that image to feed me now as a solitary so that I wouldn't hunger. But it couldn't. I was no longer a child, but an adult.

As time passed, I began to see the solitude itself as Eucharistic food.

I had a prayer vision once. I was in a cave. Behind me was a vast entrance. Before me was an inscrutably black impassible rock wall—God. On the floor was a torch that looked like a flashlight. Out of it poured liquid light. This light illumined the cave wall. With it, I could see the endlessly fascinating texture of this unknowable God. For years, I wondered what this "light" was—was it Jesus? Was it the Holy Spirit? Was it a call for me to write? It wasn't until I cradled the torch in my lap one day in prayer that I realized I was holding the Christ Child before he became Child. And that I—and others—could eat and drink this light.

In this sense, God becomes the mother, and feeds, in another way, the solitary. The hermit eats the presence of God. She drinks it. She is like an opening, a mouth, into which the unknowable pours in—a portal unable to resist God's desire to enter into humanity.

Such an interpretation argues that the solitary is fed differently from others. To trust that I am fed by this mystical Eucharist is too frightening for me right now. Moreover, I question anything that separates me from my community. The Eucharist is the physical form of food that allows the believer to feed on God, to partake of the incarnate mystery of love. I have as much need for that food as any other Christian.

I began to define, and struggle with, a concept of obedience that is far more complex and difficult than I ever anticipated. Which obedience took precedence: honoring solitude, or honoring Eucharist with my community?

The solitary, I have begun to realize, sees community from the opposite side of the mirror—a perfect, but reverse, reflection. The Church teaches that Christians come together in physical community to share the meal that *defines their union with God*—Eucharist. The solitary, *living in the mystical presence of God*, needs to eat Communion to define her union with community.

The Eucharist binds a people to God in community. But God chooses how to bind each person into that community. Some are bound by preaching, some by teaching, some by healing. Some bring their gifts of parenting, service, working against injustice. And sometimes, God binds a person into solitude for the sake of the community.

If the Church defines the community eligible to receive Communion as the physical community gathered under one roof, then the solitary will be an outcast. If the Church defines community as a commitment to each other, then the solitary is, by definition, profoundly part of that community and must be fed.

The Eucharistic hunger, which drove me into the arms of the Church, has never gone away. If anything, the deeper I commit to solitude, the greater it becomes. Sometimes I feel the vocation is too hard, too lonely. I do not want to stay in the mystery that solitude invites one to *without* the daily sustenance of Communion. Sometimes I disbelieve I have the call or the courage. But it has been five years since I began to live in solitude. There comes a time when you accept the unusualness of your vocation because the struggle to fight it becomes too exhausting. I have reached that point.

Today's Church has no provision for private Communion. It remembers too keenly the priests who held private Mass for themselves, elevating their spirituality above the people they served. The adoration of the Blessed Sacrament, requests by laity to reserve the Sacrament in their homes—all of this can easily slip into an exclusive, excluding form of worship that is utterly contrary to Jesus' eating and drinking with tax collectors and prostitutes, and constantly urging us to community in the table fellowship of a meal.

I am not unaware of these problems, but I believe the Church starves a vital resource in its midst.

Thus, at the deepest level, obedience is a mystery to me. I believe, with an insistence that surprises and almost frightens me, that obedience *is* to honor the obligations of my own life—which is solitary—over my own preferences for community. So for six days I hunger; on the seventh, I am fed.

For me, this is the dark side of saying an obedient "yes" to solitude. In times of frustration, God seems the tyrant, tying me to an unwanted vocation—one I would never choose for myself. I want a visible ministry. I want a romantic version of the Christian life—one from which I will receive approval and confirmation from my Church and my friends. Instead, I have *this:* a hope—and nothing more.

*   *   *

Defining obedience for oneself cuts through theological issues, psychological issues, and personal issues. While the issue of Eucharist forced me deep into Church theology, my attempts to structure a daily lifestyle were clearly influenced by psychological and personal issues.

When I began a solitary life, I decided the endless hours of aloneness needed to be structured. I was fearful that my laziness and self-indulgence would make a mockery of my vocation. So I defined a daily structure that included prayer and meditation, reading, writing, and physical labor. While I did not read any rules of religious life, I am sure similarities exist.

When one faces a long and blank day, and wants to be "religious," these elements immediately come into play.

Accordingly, I divided my day into hours of prayer, religious reading, writing, and lastly (and inadequately) physical labor. Slowly I put the corset of hours around me, and daily tightened its grip around my solitary life. I cinched it with determined fingers, sure it was pleasing to God. God wanted solitude; I would give it wrapped in as much holiness as I could muster. I was so awed by the special call to solitude, I overreacted.

Then came the month-long trip out West with a Carmelite sister, older and wiser than me. She *never* seemed to follow a formula or a pattern. We set aside some time (a very limited time) for our devotions. She always remembered her community; she always prayed the psalms—but not necessarily the ones prescribed for that day; and we celebrated Communion. And that was that.

Then she raptured about nature. She marveled at the sequoias; she raved about the sea; she became ecstatic over snow-dusted mountain tops. There was no discipline to her day, no sacrifice to God, no inner listening to obey. She simply became one with the day and its beauty.

It was not a holy life—according to my ritually structured day—but a gleeful, childlike one.

When I came home, I put all my books away. The Liturgy of the Hours. The rosary. The Gospel readings for the day. The lives of St. Teresa, and St. John, and St. Therese. And I ordered, as I recall, three pallets of stone and built a stone wall in my backyard.

*   *   *

Obedience is a willingness to be carried by the wind. It is a willingness to let go of our definition of faith-filled obedience filled with illusions and superstitions. My neatly ordered day with its rituals was a silk-lined coffin into which I pressed the image of a religious person, a corpse with hands in a death grip on her rosary and religious books. I was obedient only to my own illusion.

I have left that behind and entered a radically different world.

What is "obedience" for me today?

I listen to life. I attend to it like a loving mother. I listen to the pulse of it; the heartbeat of it. I *feel* life—in all of its textures, its

pains, its incredible beauty, its sorrow. When I am with someone, I want his or her story in my heart. Often what I feel is
wordless, unable to be spoken. Sometimes I feel God working
in those stories—no matter how painfully—and no words seem
necessary. Most of the time, I see people doing what I also have
done. They obey some internalized book of rules unknown to
anyone but themselves.

It is hard for God to enliven a life already frozen in sanctity.

Obedience is obeying the sacred rhythm within *you*. Not the
ego rhythm, but the sacred rhythm. The ego leaves a few heavy-
footed clues. For me, my warning signals are when I try to take
an inspiration and transform it into an interpretation. The inspiration to be solitary becomes the interpretation of rules and
a rigid regime.

There is short-term satisfaction in self-defined obedience,
but a long-term sense of failure. While I felt better about myself
being obedient to my definition of obedience, the world was
narrower and more rigid. I always worried. *Should I be trying
harder? Should I be doing more for God? Am I being obedient to
God?* I boxed myself in with disciplines; and then I was liable to
them for obedience—or disobedience. I could feel the solitude
within me becoming sterile.

Now I have a healthy respect for obedience. It is far more
subtle than my heavy-handed interpretation. It requires far
more trust. It is our insecurity that makes us grasp rules as a
holy grail. It is harder to have such profound trust in the Holy
Spirit within ourselves that we simply *live* an enjoyable solitary
life waiting, somewhat childlike, for whatever. And always, always being ready to leave.

I imagine the worst sin of the solitary life is to presume it is
forever. That is an obedience that allows for no new inspira-

tion, no new breath of the Spirit. Perhaps the call is a lifelong call. But perhaps it is a time-out, a pause between active chapters. To presume to know is to block out the validity of God.

It would be sad to miss the beauty of solitude because one is always worrying about being obedient to the call of solitude. Now that I have loosened my grip on the rigidly structured obedient life, the dawn nurtures me; the silence feeds me; the solitude strengthens me; the solidarity with the poor comforts me; and the obedience—my assumption that God will guide when guidance is called for—grounds me.

Obedience is allowing what is to become what it wishes to be—in myself and others. For good or for bad. To be unafraid. To know that there can be great pauses between movements in one's life. To accept times when no inner voice is heard; times when only silence—immutable silence—*is* the guidance offered.

I thought once that if I took on this daunting vocation of solitude, that God owed me continuing conversation and dialogue. When God fell utterly silent, I succumbed to fear, anger, distress, anxiety, gloom, uncertainty—and yet the silence went on.

Then I loosened up. I just gave up my hope, and built a stone wall. I did whatever helped me get through the silence while staying in the silence. I enjoyed myself. If a poem helped, I wrote a poem. If music helped, I put on a CD. I simply enlarged the silence and solitude until it became bearable.

I am not sure what God "wants" from the solitary—if God wants anything at all. It may well be that it is sheer gift. Perhaps God says, "She is a bit frazzled. She needs to be alone. I'll put the seed of solitude within her. There, I know, she'll flourish."

And I, in being obedient, am simply allowing God to make me more beautiful.

Prayer

To Be in God's Presence Always

There is, perhaps, too much said about prayer. It implies a need for humans to "talk" to God, to have some sort of conversation. Because we are relational, we impose a certain chattiness upon God.

We talk; we kneel; we quiet our hearts. We read innumerable books on how to pray, and always, we are told it is important to our spiritual life.

Because of so much importance placed on prayer, we devote considerable emotional energy to resolving our dissatisfaction with our efforts—and the results. We treat prayer as though it were a debutante meeting the Queen. We believe we must pray with perfect comportment, and bow with angelic beauty and grace.

Still, in spite of our best and labored efforts, rarely is there a sense of intimacy with God. So how is one to "be in God's presence always"?

When I first began a solitary life, I placed *great* importance on prayer. It was for this I was destined. The hermit prayed. The hermit—having no job in the workaday world—devoted hour after hour of uninterrupted attentiveness to the immutable, often silent God. And surely, the religious traditions have all reinforced this, from monastic to Buddhist.

A dilemma, however, immediately presented itself. I was not cloistered, nor was I a cave dweller. I lived on a suburban street in mainstream America. My phone rang, often incessantly. I had children. I was Catholic—and expected to attend Mass. I had friends and family.

The call to silence was not validated by anyone other than myself. It became the greatest struggle I would face in my desire to become a silent dweller. And the crux of that struggle centered on prayer itself.

Initially, I hungered for union with God—the desire of every mystic. It seemed the pinnacle of the spiritual journey. I avidly read the mystics' stories from Julian of Norwich to St. John of the Cross. I felt I had the same yearning within me, and often in prayer I sensed that timeless spaciousness that hinted at such union with the Divine.

I sensibly thought that this lifestyle—one of silence and solitude—would allow me to throw myself into the arms of my invisible Beloved. Though I did not like the word "espoused"—I was too modern a woman for that—I yearned for that oneness, that union.

St. Teresa of Ávila often spoke of the spiritual journey. It began, for all seekers, by hard work. She likened it to hauling water from the well to the garden. As one's journey progressed—in God's time, not our own—rain began to fall on the garden, so much that the gardener was sometimes nearly drowned. God raptured those faithful to the task of prayer—though when and how were never to be known.

So I began. With morning, midday, and evening times of prayer. Written devotions, silent meditation. I directed my attention toward God. During the rest of the day, I worked quietly at my tasks of writing, cleaning, and attended to my children's needs and the outer world in general.

I was clearly a woman hauling water from the well to the garden.

While I was directing my energy in one direction, however, silence was growing within me. Just silence. Not some euphoric experience. Not mystical union with God. But a quietness that was very comforting, that felt complete in itself.

It grew and grew, without any structured attention on my part. I did not try to be silent. I have more the nature of an extroverted talker than a quiet introvert. But, because I spent hours and days alone, quietness had a place to grow of its own accord within me. Until one day I noticed it.

I was walking my greyhound in the nearby park—something I did every morning and evening. And I was thinking about how poorly I prayed. I wondered if I would ever become the mystic I wanted to be. I wondered if I would ever have this coveted union I felt such a hunger for within myself.

It was a quiet morning, a beautiful one. And I was very content with the beauty of silence. It had grown from a word—something needed for prayer life—to a sturdy, dependable, comforting inner companion. No matter where I went, no matter how frazzled I was, beneath all I felt an inner security grounded in this silence.

It occurred to me at that moment that I was not meant to be a mystic. I was never meant for that. My path was simply to dwell in silence. I would not have mystical intimacy with God. I would have the lowly reliable companion of silence for my life's journey. I was looking high to the heaven for meaning in my life—to be a contemplative woman of prayer. And the answer was found on the ground beneath my feet—the solid comfortable presence of silence.

It was then that I became, in my own mind, no longer a hermit or a solitary, but a silent dweller.

I no longer pray much, in the traditional sense. I attend to the morning, still, in a prayerful way. I find it important to ground myself in God's love and mercy. But I believe God wants to be with me in the way of ordinary silence. I believe I have union with God, though it is a simple one, accessible to all of us.

I simply live in silence. I wonder, to my utter surprise, if what I have called silence has actually been Spirit. This silence is so unassuming, yet so faithfully present. It does not ask me to quiet my racing mind or disown my selfish thoughts. It does not say I must put on the straitjacket of mindful presence, or meditation, or directed prayer before it will sit with me. With silence, I do not find myself strangling in self-condemnation over feelings of inadequacy. I am not angry at God for being expected to be still and mindful, to wait and listen when I want to scream: "But THIS is what I need to be with, right now. This *is* who I am."

Silence simply holds the whatever-is-in-me in an accepting embrace, and allows it to unfold and speak its truth within me. I always feel reverenced and loved when I am allowed simply to *be* in my own body, in silence.

About eight years ago, I was introduced to a process called Biospiritual Focusing by two priests, Ed McMahon and Peter Campbell, both psychologists who specialize in the psychology of spirituality. They called it a way of being with what is real inside ourselves at any given moment, without judgment. We were taught to use the process with a partner; but eventually we learned to self-focus.

It has become prayer.

"To be in God's presence always" means that we must be authentically ourselves in God's presence. We cannot divorce ourselves from ourselves through some recommended prayer practice. After having practiced centering prayer, meditation, and even experienced many profoundly moving moments of contemplative joy in the living presence of God, I trust Biospiritual Focusing as the surest road to travel.

It allows me to stay with myself as I am at any given moment—in the holy context of inward, grace-attended, listening silence. I listen to how I *feel* within my body. The icky creepy feeling, the tight suffocating feeling, the bubbling euphoric feeling—those body feelings are who I am at that moment when I open myself to the presence of God.

In the Christian tradition, we have been asked to quiet our minds. This is a good thing. Our minds are engineered to be analytical, to process data. Our brain is a complex sensory organ. It is designed to take raw data from the five senses and direct our response. It is not so much soulful as mind-*full*. It can take soul data and help us find a real life-directed response; but it cannot *generate* soul data.

However, many of us quiet not only our minds but tune out our bodies too. We believe we are called—during prayer—to relinquish the heavy sorrow we are carrying, the rage we are feeling, the confusion that beleaguers us. We believe that, during prayer, we are standing on holy ground and we must cleanse ourselves not only of our chattering thoughts but our body-felt feelings. Thus, we "listen" to God's word in our life. We put ourselves into a totally passive listening presence, and wait. And wait. And wait. For God to stir the waters within us, to comfort us, to guide us, to simply *be* with us in a moment of contemplative union.

We come *incomplete* before God. We have left the essential parts of ourselves behind, like sandals left outside the Temple. Yet those sandals are what we walk on all day long. They are what cradle our vulnerableness through life. We need to find a way to bring our sandals *into* the Temple of prayer.

In Biospiritual Focusing, we stand in our sandals. We have this strange sense that the holy solution for the next step on our journey is within our bodies, and accessible to us because God is completely incarnate in us. God calls us to wholeness, which *is* holiness. We are called to be completely human in the best sense of that word. We are not yet angels. We eat; we tire; we get angry; we make love. The gift God has given us is the gift of human *life*. It is a fixed, time-limited gift with a beginning and an end. Our holy job is to embody, on earth, the love that is God, as completely as we can.

Prayer is our only hope, but not a prayer that divorces us from our human nature but one that embraces it. To be continuously in the presence of God is to be continuously in the very real presence of our own body in a caring way. It is knowing that God is incarnate in my very flesh, cell by cell. I am *imprinted* with merciful Love. I can feel it within my own flesh, and it is pure grace.

The task, in prayer, is to quiet the mind so that the body wisdom—which is our incarnated gift—can guide us. It *is* a letting go, temporarily, of our extraordinary cognitive abilities, so that the raw data of our soul can be heard.

Beneath every problem and every feeling lies the guidance of the Spirit. We have tended, as a culture and a religion, to be *outside* of ourselves for answers. We read books; we listen to authorities; we pray to a remote God. We process that data with our mind, and direct our life's course. But always, there is an edge of incompleteness. We lack an assuredness. There is something missing—like a critical piece of data.

That missing piece is the *inward* listening to our own reality.

In the rapid high-tech pace of life today, inward listening is devalued. Technology is exponentially increasing the amount of knowledge available to the human mind. We have become an information-addicted society. That is why prayer is so foreign to us. Prayer requires that we put information aside for a moment.

For an information-addicted culture, taking time to pray can actually *feel* like physical withdrawal. We get acutely uncomfortable being with ourselves in silence. To cope with the anomaly, we place prayer into a separate category of something we "must do." It becomes a chore, a necessary practice we accept because we are told it is required for salvation, for the good of the world, for our self-certainty that we are good religious people.

Because information is our basic reality, and we are most comfortable processing facts, we see prayer as external to ourselves. Naturally, we see ourselves as failures at prayer. I have heard more than one minister say, from the pulpit, that he or she *does not know how to pray*. One person prayed as he drove his car in a frenzy from one ministerial task to the next. The other simply admitted defeat.

We are also, as a culture, addicted to *doing*. We solve problems; we invent solutions. We are a take-charge society, which means we analyze data, produce a plan, and act on it. Such a process feeds on the information addiction, and it relieves the anxiety by doing something. When that doing something does not work, we look for more information, design a new solution, and take a new action. Rarely do we listen inwardly to *feel* our way toward a next step. Rarely do we trust a process that unfolds slowly. Rarely do we accept that we might not *know* how things will turn out, but trust the inward guidance—even when it seems to contradict our information-based data.

The French philosopher Max Picard noted,

> Nothing has changed the nature of man so much as the loss of silence. The invention of printing, technics, compulsory education—nothing has so altered man as this lack of relationship to silence, this fact that silence is no longer taken for granted, as something as natural as the sky above or the air we breathe. Man who has lost silence has not merely lost one human quality but his whole structure has been changed thereby.

Our culture is losing the art of silence, and with it the intrinsic human understanding and capacity for prayer. While less advanced cultures continue to preserve, naturally, the human value of silence, prayer, and gratitude, high-tech societies are rapidly disconnecting from it.

Like endangered animals confined to cages for controlled breeding, silence and prayer are at risk of becoming unnatural and artificial. Rather than being a natural part of the human rhythm, they are becoming "cultivated." Dozens of how-to-pray books have populated the bookshelves of bookstores, libraries, and homes.

Silent dwellers, by creating spacious times of physical silence in their lives, slowly recover the human capacity to be with themselves in a gentle caring way. Perhaps the farmers who plowed the fields all day long behind dray horses, and the women who kneaded dough into bread, knew quiet inward listening as instinctive to their nature. They would not have called it prayer, or Biospiritual Focusing; they probably did not call it anything at all. They simply stayed with what was inside them in the quietness of their day, and eventually it spoke to them. They felt the underlying fear or concern driving the issue. Perhaps their son was sullen, and they realized it was the anniversary of his favorite grandfather's death. Or perhaps a husband and wife were at odds, and they realized it was the concern over falling crop prices.

These may not seem to be high spiritual insights—but that is a problem of our cultural expectations of what is holy. In reality, we are called to live in harmony with ourselves and one another. That is all. That *is* the great commandment: to love one another and oneself. It is the day-to-day, moment-by-moment decisions that define that love. Love wilts if the parents rail at the sullen child; it freezes in the face of marital anger. When we listen quietly and with reverence to our own true story, it offers a solution—a way to be with how-things-are in a human holy way.

We are not angels, and most of us are not saints. We are human beings—and it is hard to be a human. Prayer is not meant to elevate us from our human condition; it is not meant to be set apart from our lives. Prayer is as ordinary as breathing.

When I began my journey into solitude, I had a very different agenda than I have today. Silence and solitude were tools I intended to use to climb a very precipitous mountain to God. I saw them as possessions rather than gifts—explorers' equipment required for a perilous expedition to God. Prayer was the amulet I clutched in the hand against my heart to protect me from harm. But determined I was to go—and conquer the mystery of God.

Oh, a touch of arrogance!

What I was doing, as improbably as it would have seemed if anyone had suggested it, was making a journey towards becoming a human. I wanted to be an angel or a saint, but the path I set would lead full circle to a human being's home—an admission that I was only a human, who with grace, had *hope* of becoming perhaps, one day, a good human.

Now, ironically, I feel closer to being in God's presence always than ever I did when I was so strenuously seeking God. It is as though I was blind, utterly blind, in my quest. But because I took silence and solitude along as companions (thought I thought them tools), no other result was possible.

It is in silence and solitude that one learns—or regains—the human quality of being in God's presence always. It is a place filled with gratitude and awe, and also one filled with day-to-day tribulations, trials, and frustrations of being human.

I no longer look outward, or to strange and exotic places or techniques or gurus, to be with God. Perhaps these are ways to God. Certainly, there are centuries of tradition supporting them. But mine is a very ordinary way. It is as close as my breath.

I breathe—into the horror and joy of being human—and find God.

Epilogue

I began this manuscript in 1997. Midway through, I put it away—never to be published. I felt very uncomfortable describing a lifestyle as though I understood it myself. Also I realized, as a writer, how words can make something seem more pure and perfect than it really is in actuality.

When I published my book *Silence*, occasionally I would receive letters from readers. One came from Jim Gerofsky in New Jersey. He had bypassed my book when he first saw it, thinking it was a how-to-be-spiritual-at-your-next-dinner-party self-help book. Eventually, however, he bought it and shared with me his own journey into solitude. As I read his profoundly moving writing, I realized he was going through some of the exact same struggles I had undergone myself.

I remember looking for a book to guide me into a modern-day experience of solitude. *Anyone's* experience would have been a consolation. I was unnerved by this insistent call into a solitary lifestyle. I sought someone who had gone before. Not a religious. Not a saint. Not a historic figure. I wanted a modern ordinary man or woman to draw comfort from, as I ventured into unknown territory.

I found nothing.

And so, I simply plunged ahead as best I could, leaning heavily on the spiritual direction I received. I was always adamant: I would leave this solitude if ever I received the same inner certainty I had gotten to enter it.

I am still waiting.

My solitude is a messy affair. Nothing holy about it. If I were to live every aspect of what I have written for even one day, I would be stunned. One day, I feel anchored in silence but hopelessly off in prayer. Another day, I will just be wretched about the dilemmas of simplicity. Often, solidarity simply gets forgotten. Completely.

Writing is like painting a picture of the *best* images, the best vision within us of what we have experienced. Yes, I have had moments of grace-infused prayer. Yes, silence is a balm to me. True, solitude has become a companion. But this life is like any life—no more sacred or holy or awesome. It has the same successes and failures as trying to be a parent, or a good teacher, or a morally ethical executive.

Like many single people, I wonder if someday a man will walk into my life and the attraction will be so compelling and rewarding that I will abandon solitude like an old unwanted dog. I will anesthetize what may be my deepest calling because of loneliness, or just sheer boredom. Or perhaps solitude is not my deepest calling, but a significant time-out so I can ready myself to be more authentically present in this world.

Two years ago, when I bought the RV, I began to travel all over the United States. Alone. I was a hermit-on-wheels. Why?

Why did I leave my hermitage—often for weeks at a time—to travel thousands of miles? How did that fit with this solitary lifestyle?

I was not escaping solitude, nor abandoning this inner call. I was seeking to console it with the incredibly comforting presence of nature. The trimmed suburban lawns and pruned trees, the tidy flower gardens and vegetable patches hemmed in my solitude. I often felt like a potted bonsai struggling for wild life.

I stayed at a state campground utterly alone on an enormous lake, insecure and somewhat frightened, but willing to be cut off and vulnerable. I drove up torturous windy two-lane roads to see ancient Indian civilizations. I traveled across the northern plains as winter snow and ice were covering the land.

And then I came home—and never wanted to move again.

All through my travels, silence, solitude, simplicity, solidarity, obedience, and prayer accompanied me—the constant ballast of my life. It has surprised and awed me that what I wrote in the Covenant years ago continues to bear fruit within my life. It is like a sturdy wall I can lean against to get my bearings.

My main change from when I began to today is this: I don't take my *image* of a solitary life seriously. Initially, I was like an artist trying to paint the most realistic vision of perfect solitude I could imagine. I wanted the light and beauty of a Vermeer painting. Now, I throw paint on the canvas of my life like Van Gogh, content to capture the essence of that momentary image—to allude to all it can be. And I can feel within myself a desire to simply paint *color* onto the canvas of my remaining life. Vibrant, joy-filled color. Dark, moody color. Waves and lines and patterns of life interwoven into a wild profusion of love.

It is strange. When I began, God and Church were synonymous. One led to the other in an endless circle. I *wanted* the God of my solitude to be defined by the Church of my faith. I wanted the written prayers, the guidance of the saints, the liturgical hours and days of the seasons to *be* my solitary lifestyle.

I never expected that instead of my conforming *more* to a life of Church-defined faith, a redefinition of faith and Church would emerge. Only in death will I understand what now perplexes me. But I feel I am coming alive. I feel my own love awakening within me. A sheltered love, one hidden yet blooming.

If living solitary has done nothing else, it has taught me that God's love is more vast, more generous, more incomprehensible than any of us could believe. I sometimes drown in the Light.

In support of their Newsletter,
fifty percent of all profits from the sale of
Silent Dwellers will be contributed to:

Friends of Silence
129 Skunk Hollow Road
Jericho, Vermont 05465

For information about
BioSpiritual Focusing, contact:

Institute for BioSpiritual Research
P.O. Box 741137
Arvada, CO 80006
Tel/Fax 303-427-5311

Website: http://www.biospiritual.org
E-mail: LFLOM@mho.net

For a quarterly newsletter devoted to the solitary life,
contact *Raven's Bread*
P.O. Box 562, Hot Springs, NC 28743
(Subscription: $7.50)

Also published by Continuum

Psalms for Praying
AN INVITATION TO WHOLENESS

NAN C. MERRILL

"A much-needed resource for home liturgies and individual prayer."—*Contemporary Spirituality*

"Merrill has reworked the Book of Psalms in a loving, contemplative manner, which betrays none of the book's original vigor or essence. Rather, in a mode that is fresh and eloquent, Merrill's psalms evoke that deep sense of reverence and soul-stirring dialogue with the divine that is often eclipsed by the fear of divine wrath in the original. Highly recommended for all libraries."—*Library Journal*

"The very liveliness of the Psalms causes us to want to say them in our own language. Nan Merrill has done this marvelously, and I'm grateful for this labor of love."—Madeleine L'Engle

Meditations and Mandalas

SIMPLE SONGS FOR
THE SPIRITUAL LIFE

NAN C. MERRILL

"The mandalas illustrating this book emerged as
daily meditations over a summer season. This motif,
symbolizing wholeness, reconciliation with the opposite, and restoration of balance and harmony, en-
hances the potential for centering us and deepening
our times of prayer. These hand-crafted mandalas
represent the fruits of my own centering prayer and
are offered as another dimension to meditation, to
be reflected upon with the heart's eye rather than an-
alyzed with the mind."—Nan C. Merrill

At your bookstore or from
The Continuum Publishing Company
370 Lexington Avenue, New York, NY 10017

www.continuum-books.com